EDUCATED

Tara Westover

*sparknotes

*sparknotes

This 2020 edition printed for SparkNotes LLC by Sterling Publishing Co., Inc.

ISBN 978-1-4114-8034-6

Distributed in Canada by Sterling Publishing Co., Inc.
c/o Canadian Manda Group, 664 Annette Street
Toronto, Ontario M6S 2C8, Canada
Distributed in the United Kingdom by GMC Distribution Services
Castle Place, 166 High Street, Lewes, East Sussex BN7 1XU, England
Distributed in Australia by NewSouth Books
University of New South Wales, Sydney, NSW 2052, Australia

For information about custom editions, special sales, and premium and corporate purchases, please contact Sterling Special Sales at 800-805-5489 or specialsales@sterlingpublishing.com.

Manufactured in Canada

Lot #:
2 4 6 8 10 9 7 5 3 1
09/20

sterlingpublishing.com
sparknotes.com

Please email content@sparknotes.com to report any errors.

Contents

Context

Tara Westover was born in rural Idaho in 1986, the youngest of seven children. She was raised in a strict Mormon family, with almost no contact with the outside world. As Tara recounts in her memoir, she did not have a birth certificate until years after she was born. Despite her isolated upbringing and lack of formal education, Tara rebelled against her parents and began studying at Brigham Young University, where she proved herself to be an academically gifted student. After graduating from BYU in 2008, Tara went on to earn a master's degree and a PhD from the University of Cambridge. She also won a Gates Cambridge Scholarship, and held a position as a visiting scholar at Harvard University.

Among Tara and her siblings, three of them have not only been able to pursue higher education, but have also completed doctorates. Tara's experience studying, exploring history, and gaining a wider perspective of the world prompted her to question some of the beliefs she grew up with, and realize that many things about her childhood had been unhealthy and damaging. In 2009, while at work on her graduate studies, Tara confronted her parents about the abuse she had been suffering for years at the hands of her brother. Their denial finally prompted Tara to sever ties with them. Once estranged from her family, Tara began to reflect on her experiences and process the trauma she endured. Mentors and friends encouraged her to tell her story, because they knew it was astonishing. Tara eventually turned this combination of narrative and reflection into a memoir, *Educated*, which was published in 2018.

Educated immediately topped the *New York Times* Best Seller list and received many positive reviews as well as numerous awards. It was named one of the Best Books of 2018 by *The New York Times*, *Oprah Magazine*, *The Economist*, *The Guardian*, and *Publishers Weekly*. Tara was chosen by *Time Magazine* as one of the 100 Most Influential People of 2019. Many critics and readers have praised Tara's honesty and vulnerability in revealing both the abuse she suffered and the sense of loss she experienced as she gradually cut ties with her family. In interviews she gave after the publication of her memoir, Tara has stated that she is only in contact with three of her siblings, and that she no longer practices Mormonism or any other religion.

In the memoir, Tara clearly states that she has to rely on memories and conflicting accounts about events that occurred a long time ago. Because her family was so isolated and avoided contact with public services at all costs, there are almost no official records for Tara to use to confirm what she remembers. Tara uses pseudonyms for many of the characters in her memoir, including both of her parents and many of her siblings. The memoir also begins with a note in which Tara states that "This story is not about Mormonism. Neither is it about any other form of religious belief." Tara attempts to reject interpretations that would present her memoir as fueled primarily by a critique of Mormonism, and she shows compassion toward the childhood she experienced. Nonetheless, some of her family members have come forward to challenge the events she recounts in the book.

A lawyer has made statements on behalf of Tara's parents, claiming that the memoir misrepresents both the quality of education Tara received while homeschooled and the severity of the injuries that were treated at home rather than in medical settings. Although the memoir is dedicated to Tara's brother Tyler—who also chose to pursue an education and inspired his younger sister to do the same—Tara has stated that Tyler disputed some of the content of the memoir after its publication.

Plot Overview

Educated is primarily retrospective, consisting of Tara Westover's memories about her past. She tells the story of the events of her life from a vantage point in her late twenties, occasionally interjecting to comment on the process of trying to arrive at an accurate version of the past. Tara was born the youngest of seven children to parents whom she refers to as Faye and Gene (pseudonyms). The Westover family lived on a farm in rural Idaho, where Gene made a living salvaging scrap metal while Faye worked as an unlicensed midwife and herbal healer. Gene suffered from paranoid fears about interference from the federal government, and, as a result, he refused to allow his children to attend school, receive birth certificates, or receive medical attention. Gene was also a devout Mormon who believed in radical self-sufficiency and an impending Day of Judgment.

Shifts in the Westover family dynamic began to emerge when Tara was about nine. Her mother's work as a midwife increased her sense of independence, but after sustaining a serious and untreated brain injury in a car accident, Faye began to lose confidence in her skills. She then focused instead on using herbal remedies and a form of intuitive healing. Around this time, Tyler (the third son) announced that he was going to attend college, which estranged him from his family. Tyler's absence forced Tara to become more involved in helping her father with his scrapping work, which left her constantly exposed to the possibility of dangerous injury. It also made her more curious about possibly pursuing an education herself. When Tara was ten, she told her disapproving father that she wanted to begin going to school, but nothing came of the idea.

As Tara grew into her teens, she acquired more independence from her family, due to taking on various jobs and pursuing singing and musical theater in the local community. However, her life was dominated by the strict rules and religious doctrine her father imposed, and Tara often worried about becoming sinful. When Tara was thirteen, her older brother Shawn moved back home. At first, Shawn and Tara were close and spent a lot of time together. When Tara was about fifteen, however, Shawn began to be physically abusive toward her. His behavior only got worse after

Shawn experienced a head injury. Tyler eventually realized that Shawn was hurting Tara, and he urged Tara to seriously consider applying to college and getting away from the family. Although she was uncertain at first, Tara began to study and was eventually accepted at Brigham Young University, having passed herself off as homeschooled.

In January 2004, when Tara was seventeen years old, she moved to Utah to begin her college education. She found the adjustment very difficult at first, but eventually began to excel in her studies. Tara's finances were precarious, and she had to hold multiple jobs and maintain very high grades to retain her scholarship. Her emerging independence also caused a threatening dynamic between her, Gene, and Shawn. Whenever Tara returned to Buck's Peak, her father manipulated her into working for him, while Shawn continued to physically and emotionally abuse her. Tara eventually confided to a bishop about her life, and he helped her to secure funding to finance her education. Tara's studies, and the people she met, also gradually opened her eyes to different realities and forced her to realize how damaging and isolating her childhood had been. Tara eventually changed her major to history and was encouraged to apply for a study-abroad program at the University of Cambridge in England.

Tara's experience at Cambridge broadened her horizons even further, and she was encouraged to consider graduate studies. Tara still felt isolated from her peers, and ashamed of her origins. She hid most of her past even from her friends and the men she occasionally dated. She was eventually awarded a prestigious Gates Cambridge Scholarship and moved to England to pursue a master's degree. She remained in close contact with her family and returned to Idaho regularly to visit, but her relationship with them deteriorated. Shawn was growing increasingly erratic and violent, and Tara feared for the safety of his wife and young child. By chance, she revealed to her sister Audrey that Shawn had been abusive to her, and Audrey later confided that Shawn abused her as well. Audrey blamed herself for not protecting her younger sister, and suggested that she and Tara confront their parents and Shawn about what happened to them.

By then, Tara had built a happy life for herself in England and was working on a PhD in history at Cambridge. However, her attempt to speak the truth quickly became a source of conflict in the family. Tara became more and more ostracized within her family, eventually culminating in Shawn learning that she had been telling their parents about the abuse she suffered. Realizing that her family would never trust her claims, Tara became estranged from most of them, with the exception of Tyler. The estrangement from her family prompted grief and depression for Tara, but she was finally able to heal, and she successfully completed her PhD. By the end of her memoir, Tara has accepted that she may never have a relationship with her family again, but she takes pride in the independence she has established and the life she has built for herself.

Character List

Tara Westover The protagonist and narrator of the memoir. Tara grows up isolated from mainstream society in a strict Mormon household and grapples with her upbringing when she later pursues her education. She is extremely intelligent and hardworking, as well as brave and physically tough. Because she grew up in a manipulative and abusive household, Tara often does not trust her instincts or judgments.

Gene Westover Tara's father, and the patriarch of the Westover household. He is devoutly religious and believes he has a mission from God. Gene also believes that he needs to be prepared for the impending apocalypse and that the government is dangerous. He is an extremely controlling man. Nonetheless, he can occasionally be loving and kind to his children. There is evidence that Gene suffers from bipolar disorder, and his mental illness may drive his paranoid delusions.

Faye Westover Tara's mother, and the wife of Gene. She grows up in a family where social conformity is highly valued and rebels by marrying Gene at a young age. She is the mother of seven children and eventually begins to work as a midwife. Later, Faye becomes well known as a healer who uses intuition to "diagnose" medical problems and treats them with herbal remedies. Faye sometimes seems willing to stand up for herself and can find sly ways of supporting Tara by going behind her husband's back. Ultimately, however, her loyalty is to her husband and her religion.

Shawn Westover One of Tara's brothers. Shawn works alongside Tara helping their father, and at times the two siblings are close. However, Shawn also flies into violent rages, especially after he suffers a serious head injury, which seems to change his personality. Beginning when Tara is a teenager, he taunts and abuses her. Shawn also displays violence toward the various women he dates, including his wife, Emily. In addition to the violence, Shawn is a skilled liar and manipulator, and he convinces the entire family to believe his word over Tara's.

Tyler Westover One of Tara's brothers. Tyler is extremely intelligent and studious, even as a young child. He is the first sibling to break with the family and pursue a college education. He eventually goes on to get a PhD and marries a woman who is much more liberal than the family he grew up in. Tyler is an ally to Tara and always tries to help his sister. He is the first person to suggest that she should move out and go to college. Tyler also believes Tara when she tells him that Shawn has abused her. Tyler is a kind and compassionate person, and he is able to find a balance between maintaining a relationship with his family and standing up for Tara.

Audrey Westover Tara's only sister. Audrey is older than Tara, and the two sisters are not close while growing up. Audrey gets married young and lives a traditional life, focused on being an obedient wife and mother. When Audrey realizes that Tara has also been abused by Shawn, she finds a sense of independence. For a brief time, Audrey is angry and wants her family to know what Shawn has done. However, Audrey is not strong enough to stand up for herself, and she quickly caves under family pressure. Audrey is much more traditional and submissive than her sister, and because she has not been educated, she cannot think for herself in the same way.

Richard Westover One of Tara's brothers. Richard is the closest to Tara in age and is also quite intelligent. He attends college and eventually gets a PhD. Richard also maintains a relationship with Tara after she becomes estranged from her family, but she is less close to him than she is to Tyler.

Charles A friend of Tara's. Charles and Tara meet when they are children and stay friends for many years, including after Tara leaves for college. Their friendship sometimes veers toward romance, but Tara is very uncomfortable with physical affection. Charles is kind, affectionate, and admires Tara. Charles is one of the first people outside of her family Tara becomes close to, but she is ashamed and desperate to hide from him the reality of the abuse she experiences. Tara eventually drives Charles away when he becomes overwhelmed and realizes he cannot save her from her problems.

The Bishop A leader in a Mormon congregation in Utah. Tara meets the bishop when she is attending college at Brigham Young University, and he can tell there is something wrong with her. The bishop is sensitive, intuitive, and kind. He takes an interest in Tara and gradually coaxes her into opening up to him. When he hears Tara's story, he never judges her, and does everything he can to try to help her.

Professor Kerry A history professor at Brigham Young University. Professor Kerry is one of Tara's teachers, and he sees her intellectual potential. He helps her get into the study-abroad program. He is a perceptive man who can see intellectual talent, and he is also committed to helping those who really need it. Although he is kind, he is somewhat naïve because he thinks Tara's insecurities simply come from her having grown up poor and uneducated.

Professor Steinberg A professor of history at the University of Cambridge. Professor Steinberg is assigned to be Tara's supervisor during her time as a study-abroad student at Cambridge. He is fascinated by her unique history and academic talent, and he is determined to see Tara go to graduate school. Professor Steinberg is skilled at solving problems to make sure that Tara can get the support she needs, and he pushes her to believe in herself.

Robin One of Tara's roommates in college. Robin takes an interest in Tara and tries to help her. She teaches Tara basic life skills, and also encourages her to do things like apply for a grant. Robin's kindness and helpfulness help Tara become more integrated into the normal world.

Emily Shawn's wife. Emily marries Shawn even though he has already been abusing her. She believes that it is God's plan for a woman to submit to her husband, and she never challenges or questions Shawn, even when he is violent to her.

Erin Shawn's ex-girlfriend. Erin gives Tara hope and the confidence to believe in herself. She confirms that Shawn abused her during their relationship, which allows Tara to believe that she is not going crazy or making up lies.

Luke Westover One of Tara's brothers. He leads a traditional life and works alongside his father.

Tony Westover Tara's oldest brother. Although he tries to live a more independent life, he ends up working for his father.

Analysis of Major Characters

Tara Westover

Tara is the protagonist and narrator of *Educated*. She changes dramatically over the course of the story, as she grows from a child into a woman and starts to understand the world around her and think critically about it. At first, Tara completely trusts what her father tells her, and she plans to live a life similar to the one she sees her parents and siblings leading. However, two main things push Tara to begin to think for herself: the harm she sees herself and her family suffering, and the education she receives as she reads, thinks, and studies. Over time, Tara sees that her family's lifestyle exposes them to physical danger and unnecessary pain. She cannot reconcile the injuries and abuse she suffers with the idea of being obedient and submissive. Her education pushes her to reflect, question, and not just follow beliefs on blind faith. Ultimately, these two experiences make it impossible for Tara to remain part of her family.

Tara's actions and choices are often conflicted because she is torn between competing motivations. On one hand, she is curious and eager to learn. She is also compassionate, so when she learns about events like the Holocaust, she realizes the harm her family's ignorance is causing. These motivations drive her toward getting educated, becoming a scholar, and expanding her view of the world. On the other hand, Tara has been socialized to please her family and obey them. She gets a sense of peace from knowing her place in the world and following the expectations of her religion. These motivations at first prevent her from totally severing ties with her family. Tara's competing motivations show why much of her character development involves a struggle to become her own person. She is eventually forced to accept that she cannot reconcile these motivations, and she chooses to engage with the world and stand up for herself.

Gene Westover

Gene functions as an antagonistic figure in the memoir because he works to thwart Tara's attempts to become her own person and think for herself. Because of his mental illness and his tendencies to be domineering, Gene always needs to be in control of everything. Whenever any of his children show signs of independence, Gene becomes very angry. He can be manipulative in his attempts to control his children, such as when he repeatedly tries to bribe and trick Tara into continuing to work for him. Gene is also motivated by his belief that he has a unique mission from God and the idea that he is invincible. He takes dangerous risks with himself and his children because he has such intense trust in his faith. Gene's sense of his divine mission is fueled even further after he survives severe burns without medical intervention.

Gene's character shows little evolution over the course of the memoir. He is never able to see beyond his stubbornness and view of the world. Tara tries to share the information she learns with him and challenge him about the assumptions he makes. Gene cannot open his mind even after Tara tells him about the abuse she has suffered. His view of the world is ingrained with his belief that men should have authority and women should be submissive. Growing older, experiencing terrible injuries, and becoming part of a very successful business do not change Gene's character. His mental illness is likely part of why he cannot evolve or learn to think differently. Although he has many flaws and is a damaging force in Tara's life, Gene also has moments of kindness. He does have the capacity to show love to his children, but he is so trapped in his paranoid beliefs that he ultimately cannot break free of them.

Shawn Westover

Shawn is a violent and threatening presence in the memoir. He is always somewhat erratic, but his behavior becomes heightened after he suffers a traumatic brain injury. Either brain trauma or perhaps inherited mental illness from his father may be motivating his violent and aggressive actions. Shawn is domineering and motivated by his drive to assert power, especially over women. He abuses Tara after she starts to show signs of independence and self-confidence. Shawn is a bully who wants to crush Tara's spirit, and he takes pleasure in breaking her spirit and getting her to submit to him. Shawn's violent behavior is consistent through the memoir: he abuses both his sisters and every woman he dates. He continues to display this pattern of behavior even after he gets married and becomes a father.

Faye Westover

Faye is a complex character whose motivations are often unclear. She maintains the appearance of being submissive to her husband because she is motivated by religious ideology. However, Faye also finds ways to sneak behind her husband's back and help her children. She repeatedly helps Tara on her path to getting an education, and sometimes she makes peace between Tara and Shawn. When Faye first learns that Tara and Audrey have been abused, she seems to side with her daughters. She shows a new side to her character because she apologizes and admits that she should have protected them. However, Faye later doubles back and reverts to her earlier submissive character. She is not brave enough to stand up to Gene and Shawn. She would rather have a peaceful home, and she is too scared to assert her independence.

Faye's career path also shows shifts in her character. When she first begins to work as a midwife, she is very timid and hesitant. As she realizes that she is a very skilled midwife, her confidence grows, and she also starts to become more assertive with her husband. However, Faye suffers a head injury in a car accident. She stops assisting at births and moves instead to creating herbal remedies. When Faye becomes more involved in herbalism, her character changes, becoming more mystical and less logical. At the start of the memoir, when she was working as a midwife, she took a scientific and rational approach to her work. After her injury, she relies on more intuitive approaches to healing. Faye does seem to have some genuine skills: she is able to provide care in situations that should be far beyond her skill set, such as when Gene is covered in burns. Faye is always able to remain calm in a crisis.

Themes, Motifs & Symbols

Themes

Themes are the fundamental and often universal ideas explored in a literary work.

The Power of Knowledge

Throughout *Educated*, the power of knowledge is depicted as the key to finding freedom and living an authentic life. When Tara first hears her older brother Tyler talk about studying and going to school, she intuitively understands that her life will be richer if she can gain more knowledge. Tara works very hard and suffers greatly in order to get her education because she realizes that her education is changing her and bringing new potential into her life. The knowledge she learns in her studies helps her to understand the world and gives her a new perspective. For example, when she learns about bipolar disorder, Tara finally understands her father's behavior and can see her family more objectively. As Tara gains knowledge, she also gains self-confidence and a sense of self-worth. Through her education, Tara finds new communities and does not solely depend on her family for her well-being.

The Instability of Memory

The instability of memory leads Tara to sometimes question her ideas about her life and feel a lack of self-confidence. Because Tara is writing a memoir and looking back to events that happened long in the past, she sometimes feels unsure about whether her memories are accurate. This problem is exacerbated because when she talks to different family members, they often have different versions of events, such as when Luke burns his leg. Tara's uncertainty about whether her memory is accurate becomes more problematic around the subject of her abuse. Her family is insistent that Tara is either confused or lying, and because Tara does not always feel confident in her own memories, she is more susceptible to doubting herself. This self-doubt is damaging to her self-worth because she never feels confident and validated.

Conflict between Identities

Many characters in *Educated* suffer from conflict between different identities, and this forces them to make difficult and painful decisions. Most notably, Tara has to choose between her identity as a devout Mormon woman who is an obedient daughter, and her identity as a thoughtful, curious person who wants to ask questions, see the world, and think for herself. This conflict causes her to suffer because she cannot reconcile these two identities, and she knows she is going to have to choose between her family and her growing identity as a scholar and a modern woman. Two of Tara's brothers, Tyler and Richard, also pursue their education and experience a similar conflict. Tyler is torn between his identity as a brother, because he wants to stand up for his sister, and his identity as a son, because he knows his loyalty might cause his family to ostracize him.

Motifs

Motifs are recurring structures, contrasts, or literary devices that can help to develop and inform the text's major themes.

Injuries

Incidents in which characters are injured occur over and over again in the memoir. Luke's leg is badly burned, Faye suffers a head injury in a car accident, Tara is also hurt in a car accident, and Gene eventually suffers very severe burns. The motif of injury makes it clear what a dangerous way of life the Westover family leads, and it reinforces how Gene's reckless choices cause harm to him and his family. These injuries signal to readers that Tara's childhood home is not a safe or sheltered place for her. While many people would assume that the role of a family is to protect and care for their children, keeping them safe from harm, Tara's parents expose their children to danger. The motif of injury also literalizes the emotional wounds Tara suffers while growing up in an abusive situation. She cannot always see how much harm is being done to her, but the motif of injury reminds readers that she is regularly being exposed to trauma.

The Mountain

The Westover family settles at the foot of a mountain called Buck's Peak. Imagery of this mountain is repeated throughout the memoir, revealing Tara's emotional bond to the place where she grew up. She describes the mountain at all different seasons and creates varying impressions of it, sometimes as a looming, threatening presence, sometimes as a source of protection. Nonetheless, the sight of the mountain always connects Tara to her past. She describes it as calling out to her and drawing her back, even at times when she is trying to move on and feel settled in other places. Tara's relationship with the mountain mirrors her relationship with her family because it is so powerful, even though it can also feel threatening. Throughout the memoir, Tara travels all around the world, and she admires the beauty of the different places she visits. Still, the only time she ever feels truly at home is when she is in sight of Buck's Peak.

Symbols

Symbols are objects, characters, figures, or colors used to represent abstract ideas or concepts.

Penicillin

While Tara is studying at college, she becomes ill and finally takes penicillin, which symbolizes her rejection of her family's values. By this point, Tara has been educated enough to understand that many of the rules her family lived by do not make sense in the modern world. She has grown up with the belief that taking medicine is bad for her, but she is tired of suffering needlessly and wants to live like a modern woman. Taking the medicine is a significant symbol that Tara is moving away from the values she was taught while growing up. The moment is so significant that Tara reaches out to tell her mother what she has done. This choice also symbolizes Tara's increasing boldness and her willingness to be honest about the woman she is becoming.

Caravaggio's *Judith Beheading Holofernes*

Caravaggio's painting symbolizes how Tara's education gradually progresses and how she becomes comfortable as an intellectual. She first sees the painting as an undergraduate in her art history class, at a time when she is struggling with her studies. With her limited experience, the violent painting—depicting a woman beheading a Syrian general—reminds Tara of someone killing a chicken. Later on, when she is a graduate student, Tara sees the painting in person while visiting Rome. By now, she has become much more educated and sophisticated, and she can appreciate the painting as a work of art. The difference between how Tara responds to the painting both times shows how far she has come, and how she has turned into someone with a much more nuanced view of the world; she can see beyond the life she lived in rural Idaho. In effect, the painting symbolizes the power of education to transform someone from being a very sheltered and limited individual to a thoughtful, cosmopolitan woman who can freely travel the world.

The Bloody Knife

When Gene tells Tara's brother, Shawn, about Tara's allegations of abuse, Shawn comes to the house with a bloody knife, which symbolizes his violent rage. Tara is not sure whose blood is on the knife, and that uncertainty makes the gesture even more menacing. Shawn uses the knife as a way to assert his dominance and power, knowing it will scare Tara. He is successful in getting Tara to say that it was all a misunderstanding and retract all her accusations. The knife symbolizes how even once Tara has spoken up and tried to stand up for herself, Shawn still wields all the power within the family dynamic. He will not back down, apologize, or try to change. He is furious that Tara dared to try to challenge him. No matter what, Shawn will always be a violent person who needs to be in control and assert his power over his younger sister.

Summary & Analysis

Prologue & Chapters 1–2

Summary: Prologue

The narrator, Tara, begins by painting a vivid picture of the setting of her childhood home, describing the farm's location near the base of a mountain in rural Idaho. She describes a memory of being seven years old and understanding that her family is different from most other families, since none of the children attended school. Tara then expands her memories to explain some key facts about her family: she is one of seven children, many of whom never received birth certificates or any formal education. She alludes to the idea of growing up expecting an apocalyptic event to someday occur. She reflects on the idea that, as a child, all of her knowledge was confined to a small region of land, and how that knowledge has proved inadequate for her as an adult.

Summary: Chapter 1

Tara begins by describing a memory she constructed out of a story she heard as child. Her father tells her and her siblings such a vivid story about the house being attacked by federal agents that five-year-old Tara becomes confused and starts to imagine that this event actually took place. Tara grows up the youngest of seven children on an isolated farm at the base of a mountain known as Buck's Peak. Her father's family has lived in this location for generations, and her father's mother, known as Grandma-down-the-hill, lives nearby. Tara's father is a deeply religious man who is also very suspicious of the government. For this reason, he does not allow any of his children to attend school. He also tells his children about an incident where federal agents shot a family who refused to send their children to school. Living in fear of an impending attack from the Feds, Tara grows up watching her family stockpile food, supplies, and weapons.

Tara's grandmother offers to take Tara away to Arizona so that she can attend school. Although Tara initially tells her grandmother that she will sneak out of the house and run away with her, she finds herself unable to leave her family.

Summary: Chapter 2

Tara recalls watching her mother begin training as an assistant to the local midwife. Tara's mother is hesitant about taking on this role, but Tara's father insists on it. Mother eventually takes over as the primary midwife in the area, which means she is kept very busy. This role gives Tara the chance to learn from the techniques her mother uses, which incorporate traditional herbal knowledge. Mother's work also gives her more financial independence and autonomy, although she is always very careful to be deferential to her husband. Mother takes an active role in eventually getting birth certificates for her four youngest children (Luke, Audrey, Richard, and Tara). When Tara is nine, she accompanies her mother to a birth for the first time. Only then does Tara fully realize that her mother is operating as an unlicensed midwife, and could face serious legal consequences if she is ever caught.

Analysis: Prologue & Chapters 1–2

The memoir opens by revealing its central conflict: Tara loves the place where she grew up, but also feels stifled by it. Buck's Peak is an almost Edenic location in that it seems free of the pressures of the outside world. Tara describes the physical world of her childhood home as stark and unforgiving, but also beautiful, and this representation reflects the dynamic with her family as well. It is tempting to quickly interpret the Westover family as bizarre or abusive because they deny their children things like birth certificates, medical care, and access to public education. Nonetheless, Tara makes it clear that her relationship with her family and her past are more complicated than that. She does not simply want to forget or condemn them; Buck's Peak, and the things she learned there, have made her who she is. However, the memoir makes it clear from the beginning that Tara's childhood was ultimately inadequate and did not prepare her for the life she wanted to lead.

Tara's recollection of her father's story about the Feds, and how it led her to confuse memory and fiction, introduces an important theme into the memoir. Part of what Tara finds challenging about sharing the story of her life is that she has to look back to the past and try to understand what actually happened. Sometimes this process is challenging because she finds her memory unreliable, or her version of events is contradicted by her other family members. However, growing up in an oppressively authoritarian family, led by a man haunted by paranoid delusions, makes navigating memories particularly complex. When she was only five years old, Tara's father started the process of presenting uncertain or fabricated events as if they were the total truth. Because Tara was young and trusting, she assumed her father's view of events was correct, and this started a process whereby she would blindly follow her father's beliefs about the world. Much of the memoir's conflict will later stem from Tara realizing that she has been fed false information about how the world really is.

When Tara's grandmother suggests that she come to Arizona and start school, this invitation foreshadows the central conflict of the memoir. While Tara's grandmother is unwilling to openly challenge her son's authority, and the way he raises his children, she shows a subversive desire to undermine the isolation he is imposing on his children. Although Tara is too young to understand it at the time, her grandmother's invitation to run away opens the possibility for her to lead a normal life and become part of society. However, because of her father's rigid and oppressive authority, this possibility has to involve secrecy and a sense of betrayal. Even though she is only a little girl, Tara has to hide her plan from her family, and cannot tell them what she is planning to do. The choice to take sides with her grandmother or her own parents reflects how, later on, Tara will always have to choose between her ambitions for the future and maintaining a close relationship with her family. Because she is still so young and vulnerable, Tara initially decides that being with her family is more important, and she loses the opportunity to lead a normal life in Arizona.

Chapters 3–6

Summary: Chapter 3

Tara dives deeper into her mother's history. Faye grew up in a middle-class Mormon family where outer appearances and social conventions were highly valued. She rebelled by marrying Tara's father, Gene. Gene grew up with an abusive father and a mother who was often busy working. His rugged, independent life was initially very appealing to Faye. Faye's family disapproved of the marriage, and during Tara's childhood, relations with her mother's family were always strained. Gene was twenty-one at the time of the marriage, and initially seemed merely rebellious and unconventional. As he aged, and the couple had more children, Gene became more and more radical, taking actions like refusing to send his children to school or installing a phone line. Tara recollects that, later in life, she learned about bipolar disorder and notes that the typical time line associated with the appearance of symptoms seems to line up with her father's gradual descent into paranoid and controlling behavior.

Summary: Chapter 4

Tara recalls a car accident that takes place when the family goes on a trip during her childhood, when she is about ten. Noticing signs of depression in her husband, Faye takes the whole family on a trip to Arizona to visit her in-laws. However, Gene spends most of the visit getting in heated arguments with his mother. Fed up, Gene insists they begin driving home, and they end up in a serious car accident while Tyler is driving. Despite the injuries, no one receives medical attention, and Faye experiences a brain injury that leads to confusion and migraines.

Summary: Chapter 5

A month after the car accident, Tyler announces that he wants to go to college. This news is especially disruptive because Tony and Shawn have also recently left home, and Gene is highly dependent on Tyler's help. Tyler has always been studious and methodical, which is uncommon in a family where most of the children receive a very haphazard education. Tara's maternal grandparents applaud this decision, but, at the time, Tara doesn't understand why her brother would want to go to school. Her interactions with her grandparents from this time period reveal that Tara sees the world from her father's perspective, and takes pride in being different.

Summary: Chapter 6

As Tara and her siblings grow older, the family dynamic continues to change. Audrey begins to work and uses her earnings to fuel her own independence. Richard and Tara also become more involved in helping their father with his job working with scrap metal. This is dangerous, fast-paced work, and Tara realizes that she is going to be in physical peril for as long as she does it. In the meantime, Faye is still suffering from the effects of her brain injury, and it makes her question her abilities as a midwife. She shifts away from working as a midwife to concocting blends of essential oils, which she believes have healing properties. Faye also seems to be moving away from a formerly scientific and rational perspective toward one where she relies on intuition and spiritual claims.

Tara's knowledge that Tyler has chosen to go away to attend school makes her more curious about education, and she finds herself daydreaming about possibly going to school herself. Richard also seems to be displaying similar tendencies, sneaking off to read and study by himself. Toward spring, Tara is involved in a dangerous accident while scrapping with her father. Her mother treats her injuries at home, rather than taking her to a doctor. A short time later, Tara tells her father that she wants to go to school, but she backs down when she sees his disapproval.

Analysis: Chapters 3–6

Because Tara is writing the memoir as an adult, she can look back and see how information like the symptoms of mental illness may have impacted her childhood. When Tara was very young, she assumed that her family was normal because they were the only family she had ever been exposed to. This experience is typical for most children, and because Tara's life was so isolated, the effect was even more dramatic. Tara's knowledge of the symptoms and typical progression of bipolar disorder is an example of how her education gives her new understanding and clarity about her early life. If she had not eventually gone away to college, she might never have learned about mental illness, and she might have always assumed that her father was right about the way he saw the world. While Gene seems unique and different from other people, his symptoms are such textbook examples of a disorder that Tara can immediately see the connection as soon as she learns about the disease. The context of mental illness is also very important because it helps to explain why Tara does not present her father as a bad person. Instead, she shows him as someone who was suffering and could not get help, because everyone around him was too isolated and ignorant to know what was happening.

Faye's injury in the car accident reflects how Gene's reckless behavior has serious, long-term consequences for his family members. Gene's impatience and bad temper lead to the family starting their drive at an unsafe time, and Tyler is a young and inexperienced driver. Part of why Gene is such a dangerous character is because he combines absolute authority with reckless and impulsive decisions. He insists on everything within the family being done according to his will, but he does not have good judgment. Faye's head injury seems to have both physiological and psychological consequences, since it robs her of the confidence to practice a profession that gave her some measure of autonomy and self-confidence. Without her work as a midwife, she reverts into being more submissive to her husband, and less able to think for herself. Part of how this change manifests is that she becomes reliant on her intuition and faith-based healing. Previously, Faye's work as a midwife made use of scientifically sound medical techniques, and she was not afraid to take a client to the hospital if the situation became dangerous. Perhaps because she knew she was using her skills as best she could, Faye's work as a midwife also seemed to increase her independence and assertiveness. Once she begins to work more with herbs, Faye's focus is much less scientific.

Tyler's decision to pursue an education represents a moment where Gene starts to lose control over his children, and sets events into motion that will eventually lead to Tara pursuing her own studies. When his children are very young, Gene uses his authority to make them live according to what he wants. As they grow older, all the children seek independence in different ways. For Audrey, Tony, and Shawn, this means looking for work beyond the family business and trying to become financially independent, but Tyler chooses a different path. He values intellectual freedom, not just financial freedom, and he knows that the only way he can gain a more complex understanding of the world is by leaving Buck's Peak and seeking out an education. Tyler's decision makes him a new type of role model for Tara: for the first time, she sees someone making choices motivated by values of curiosity and a desire to learn. Although she is not yet strong enough to strike out on her own, Tara's own sense of curiosity and independence is activated by watching her older brother. Tyler has always been studious, so the decision to go to college is a natural extension of his personality, but it marks a more distinctive departure point for Tara.

Chapters 7–11

Summary: Chapter 7

Tara describes an incident that happened during the summer months, almost a month after Tyler left home. Her seventeen-year-old brother Luke spills gasoline on his jeans, and then accidentally sets himself on fire. Panicking, he causes the fire to spread from his clothing to the dry grass of the surrounding area. The incident occurs a short distance away from the house, and Tara is alone when her brother arrives, screaming in pain from his burns. She does what she can to help him, submerging his leg in ice and water. Her mother eventually comes home and treats the burn herself despite the severity of the injury, and Tyler's intense pain.

Tara breaks from the memory to tell the reader that writing down the memory causes her to realize something. Since Luke had set the grass on fire shortly after he was injured, she wonders who put out the fire and prevented it from consuming the surrounding area. She wonders whether it is possible that Luke was with their father when he set his pants on fire, rather than alone as she has always assumed. Tara asks her brother Richard, who tells her that he remembers the story of their father sending his burned son back to the house alone so that he could put out the fire before it spread. In Luke's memory, he was with their father when the injury happened, but Gene took him back to the house and helped him before then going back to deal with the fire.

Summary: Chapter 8

By age eleven, Tara is eager to get away from working at the scrap-yard, so she begins babysitting in the nearby town. One of her clients, Mary, is a skilled pianist, and Tara learns to play piano in exchange for her services. Mary suggests that Tara also start taking dance lessons, and Tara's mother helps her to do so while hiding the lessons from her father. It is not until the day of Tara's Christmas recital that Gene hears his daughter has been dancing, and both parents go to watch Tara perform. Afterward, knowing Gene will be outraged, Tara's mother pretends to have been shocked by the recital and the costumes.

Since Tara can no longer study dance, her mother takes her to voice lessons instead. When Tara sings a hymn at church one day, she receives a lot of praise, and her father shows real pride in her talents. When Tara's voice teacher suggests that she audition for a role in a local production of *Annie*, Gene is surprisingly supportive.

Summary: Chapter 9

Tara's role as Annie takes place in the summer of 1999, shortly before she turns 13. Her father is preoccupied with his belief that January 1, 2000 will create chaos and collapse, and he focuses all of the family's energy on preparing and stockpiling. Meanwhile, Tara's success in her role as Annie leads her to continue to act and sing, although she always feels uncomfortable and ill at ease with anyone outside of her family. Through her performing, she meets a boy named Charles who is friendly to her. Gene uncharacteristically gets cable TV for the family, and Tara wonders if this is a sign that he anticipates the end is coming with New Year's. However, on New Year's Eve, Gene is astounded to find that none of his convictions come to pass, and the world continues on as normal.

Summary: Chapter 10

After New Year's, Gene lapses into a depression, so Faye plans another family trip to Arizona. Once again, the family is involved in a car accident on the way home, while driving under dangerous conditions. Tara suffers a neck injury. A short time after the accident, her older brother Shawn moves home again to help her father.

Summary: Chapter 11

To Tara's surprise, Shawn seems to take an interest in her life. He helps her to tame a horse she plans to ride, and he also drives her to her theater rehearsals. Shortly before Tara turns fifteen, Shawn comes to her aid in a dangerous situation when she is almost thrown off her horse.

Analysis: Chapters 7–11

Luke's burns reveal how much danger and suffering the Westover parents expose their children to. Gene willingly puts his children in harm's way to run his business. While injuries could happen to anyone, the way the Westover parents respond to them is really where they show their failing to offer the care they should. Even though Tara is still a child herself, she is left alone to cope with a traumatic situation. On one hand, this experience likely fosters her sense of resilience and independence, which will serve her later in life. On the other hand, it leaves her feeling utterly alone and unprotected. At the moment when Tara most needed help, there was no one there for her, and she had to do the best she could. Even when Faye does come home and finds out what has happened to her son, her decision to treat Luke's injuries herself reflects an utter disregard for his safety and well-being. His burns are very severe and he should certainly have received medical treatment as well as pain relief, but Faye and Gene put their own values ahead of their child's well-being.

Tara's confusion about the day of Luke's injury reflects the complexity of relying on memories to tell stories about the past. The very act of returning to the memory years after it happened causes her to see new angles and question the interpretation she has always had. Because Tara does not want to blindly assume that her preexisting beliefs are correct, she engages in a process of fact-checking and research to try to learn from the perspectives of others.

This choice, and Tara's decision to mention the multiple conflicting accounts of the day, show the kind of integrity and responsibility she is trying to use in writing her memoir. While her account will always be subjective and primarily driven by what she experienced and felt, Tara attempts as best she can to be balanced and fair in the stories she tells.

Tara's involvement in musical theater gives her skills that will support her independence and growth, and also allows a new side of Gene's character to be revealed. Because she has not yet gone to school or done any work outside of the family business, Tara's music lessons and performances represent the first time she has significant interactions with people outside of her own family. She starts to see that there are many different kinds of people in the world, and that many of them hold values that are very different from the ones she has seen modeled in her family. Tara's musical and acting ventures also show her that if she works hard, she can achieve her goals and excel at things. Surprisingly, Gene admires his daughter's talents, and wants to help her succeed. These tendencies show that he is not inherently a cruel person, and that he does love Tara; his love is just in conflict with his need to be in control, and his limited vision of what an acceptable life for a young woman could look like.

The focus on Shawn and Tara's sibling relationship hints that Shawn is going to be a significant character in the narrative. Up until this point, Tara has not mentioned much about her interactions with her siblings, and because Shawn initially leaves home when she is quite young, Tara does not seem close to Shawn. When Shawn returns, his attention is flattering to Tara. As the youngest in a large family, she is used to being ignored or not taken seriously. Shawn also initially appears as a protector who easily fulfills his role as elder brother. He supports Tara and keeps her safe. This initial context is important because of what will come later in Shawn and Tara's relationship; it shows that, at least for a time, Shawn is mostly kind and caring toward his sister.

Chapters 12–14

Summary: Chapter 12

Tara accompanies Shawn when he temporarily takes over his brother Tony's trucking business. During this period of closeness, Shawn playfully nicknames Tara "Siddle Lister." During one of Tara's rehearsals, Shawn and Tara meet a girl named Sadie, who clearly develops a crush on Shawn. Shawn is sometimes flirtatious with Sadie, but he also seems to be cruel to her. One day, when Shawn shows Tara the same bossy attitude he uses with Sadie, she rebels and dumps a glass of water on his head. Shawn becomes infuriated and physically hurts Tara, forcing her to apologize. Afterward, she concludes that the incident has not affected her, but retrospectively reflects that the incident was deeply traumatic.

Summary: Chapter 13

By this point in the narrative, it is 2001, and Tara's sister Audrey has gotten married, and her father is warning of an impending holy war that he sees approaching in the future. At fifteen, Tara's body is changing, and she becomes increasingly aware of the way her father criticizes women who wear revealing clothes or do anything to draw attention to themselves. Tara's friend Charles has confided that he has a crush on Sadie, and after Sadie and Shawn break up, Charles and Sadie go on a date. Shawn flies into a jealous rage, threatening Charles. He seems to be displaying increasingly violent and erratic behavior.

The next morning, Tara awakes to Shawn attacking her and calling her terrible names. Her mother tries to defend her, but has difficulty doing so. Unexpectedly, Tyler comes home and intervenes in the conflict between his brother and sister. He helps Tara to flee. When she returns home, Shawn apologizes to Tara and explains that he is just trying to protect her and save her from becoming sinful. Tyler, however, urges Tara to make a plan to leave, and suggests that she consider applying to college. The next day, Tara installs a lock on her bedroom door.

Summary: Chapter 14

Tara's father expands his construction business, with Shawn working alongside him. Shawn is often angry about his father's refusal to modernize and use safer and more efficient equipment. Meanwhile, Tara is busy with a job she has taken with a local salesman, who introduces her to the internet and cell phones. Tyler keeps pressing the issue of his sister going to school, suggesting that she could study music. Tara eventually becomes intrigued and starts to study for the ACT exam, which she will need to take as part of the college admissions process. However, Tara struggles with learning trigonometry, and finally Tyler helps her. He is about to graduate from an engineering program and plans to go on to complete a PhD at Purdue University.

After her study session with Tyler, Tara receives a phone call that Shawn has been in an accident. She later learns from Luke and her brother-in-law Benjamin that Shawn fell more than twenty feet onto a concrete wall. He initially seemed uninjured, but starts behaving strangely and aggressively about twenty minutes later. As Luke, Benjamin, and Gene try to restrain Shawn from attacking them, he hits his head on the ground a second time. Whatever happens at this point is so alarming that someone calls 911, and Shawn is airlifted to a hospital.

Tara is initially hesitant to visit Shawn at the hospital because she fears what emotions will surface, but she feels only pity when she finally visits him. Shawn is rushed home as soon as possible and continues to recover there. He and Sadie reunite, and Tara devotes herself to caring for her brother while also progressing in her studies. However, Shawn shows even more violent and erratic tendencies after his injury.

Analysis: Chapters 12–14

Shawn's abusive behavior toward Tara seems to be triggered by her increasing independence and maturity. Like his father, Shawn needs to have complete control and exert his authority at all times. He seems to be particularly triggered by women disrespecting his authority, since, as his comments to Tara reveal, he does not respect or trust women. Shawn thinks women are inherently sinful and need to submit themselves to masculine authority; as Tara undergoes puberty, she shifts in his mind from a little girl he needs to take care of to a woman whom he wants to control and dominate. The first time Shawn physically lashes out at Tara is because she will not show him the same subservience he has come to expect based on the young woman he is dating. Tara does not feel the need to do everything a man tells her to do; perhaps she resists because of the independence she has gained while performing, or because she has watched her mother develop her own skills. Shawn will not tolerate Tara's assertiveness or rebellion, and he wants to make it clear that he can dominate her physically, just as her father has always dominated her psychologically.

While it is unclear whether it changes his personality, Shawn's accident shows that the Westover siblings are leading a dangerous life. Despite the fact that his initial fall is clearly severe, no one calls for help until Shawn's second collapse, which shows that the other men are more focused on respecting Gene and his values than ensuring that Shawn gets the help he needs. Taking Shawn to the hospital represents a desperate compromise that would only be undertaken under very dire circumstances. Tara's uncertainty about whether the brain injury impacted Shawn's behavior reveals that she is unclear about how much responsibility to assign to her brother. She seems to be at least partially tempted to blame Shawn's subsequent violence on the injury he suffered, because that would make Shawn less culpable. At the same time, Tara is forced to admit that Shawn was already being abusive before the injury, which means he likely would have hurt her no matter what.

While one brother is making Tara's life hell, her other brother becomes a force urging her toward independence. Tyler seems to know that he cannot control Shawn's behavior, or change the way his brother treats Tara. Instead, Tyler focuses on supporting Tara's independence, and he knows that the best way for her to break free of her family involves expanding her education. Tyler's choice to urge Tara to go to college and get away—rather than confronting Shawn or their parents—does shift the burden of changing her life onto Tara herself. By this time, Tara is so entangled with her loyalty to her family and their values that she is hesitant to pursue Tyler's plan. Her hesitation about whether to seriously consider college shows that the abuse she is experiencing is eroding her self-confidence and making her feel unworthy. However, her love for music finally persuades her to start working toward a new goal.

Tara's road to getting an education does not begin easily. She has some basic knowledge but she has to significantly retrain her mind to take in information in a new way. She also has to grapple with learning skills that have no immediate applicability. Growing up on the farm, Tara has only ever had to learn manual labor and practical tasks. Trigonometry (and other academic subjects) is the first truly intellectual work she has had to do, and this is part of why she finds it so challenging. Nonetheless, Tara also takes a certain satisfaction and pride in the hard work, and building her confidence in what she is capable of.

Chapters 15–18

Summary: Chapter 15

As time passes, Tara becomes more uncomfortably aware that establishing her own identity will require her to rebel against her father and his controlling behavior. After her father warns her again about pursuing college studies, Tara tells her mother that she doesn't think she will go to school after all. Surprisingly, her mother is insistent that Tara ought to go. Tara continues her studies while also helping her father with his scrapping work. She takes the ACT test, but does not feel confident, and resigns herself to living the life her father wants her to have.

Noticing that Tara is saving money, her father starts charging her for various household contributions, and on the day her ACT scores arrive, he abruptly tells her to move out. At first her mother agrees, but she relents when Tara emphasizes that she is only sixteen. Shawn goes back to work and defends Tara when her father demands that she work on a dangerous machine known as the Shear. The confrontation between father and son shows that Shawn is getting increasingly fed up with his father, but, in the end, both Shawn and Tara end up working together on the dangerous machine.

SUMMARY: CHAPTER 16

> *After that night, there was never a question of whether I would go or stay. It was as if we were living in the future, and I was already gone.*
>
> *(See* QUOTATIONS, *p. 49)*

As the months pass, more and more conflicts develop between Shawn and Gene. Tara is studying to retake the ACT, hoping she can improve her score. The summer before Tara turns seventeen, Shawn is in a motorcycle accident. Tara is the only family member present and she calls her father to ask what she should do. Gene tells her to bring Shawn home. Tara loads Shawn into the car, intending to drive him home, but at the last minute she changes her mind, and takes him to the hospital instead. In the end, Shawn's injury is not as bad as it appeared, and his parents bring him home. Tara knows this decision to disobey her father marks a fundamental change in their relationship.

Three weeks later, Tara receives notice that her second ACT test has earned a score high enough to make her a competitive applicant to Brigham Young University. She immediately gets a new job working at a grocery store and submits her college application with Tyler's help. She is quickly accepted and is scheduled to start college studies in January. She will be only seventeen. Tara and her mother try to find an apartment, but Tara is too overwhelmed to do much else in preparation for her education.

Summary: Chapter 17

Tara moves to Utah, where she will be living with two roommates, Mary and Shannon. Although both girls are also Mormon, they are much less rigid about their faith, which Tara finds shocking. When she begins her classes, Tara realizes that she had not understood that there were different levels of classes, and she struggles to get into freshman-level courses. Tara is uncomfortably aware that most of her course content makes no sense to her. In this unfamiliar environment, Tara finds herself more drawn to the clarity of the faith and traditions she grew up with.

One day, in art history class, Tara asks what the word *Holocaust* means. Everyone assumes she is joking around, and they respond coldly. After the class, Tara researches the word, and is horrified and shocked to realize her ignorance. Tara begins to disagree with her roommates about her commitment to keeping the Sabbath very strictly.

Summary: Chapter 18

Tara realizes that she seriously underestimated the expenses of attending college and wonders how she will be able to continue to afford it. Her academic performance is nowhere strong enough to win a scholarship, and she struggles in particular with her Western Civilization course. As Tara wrestles with frustration about her strange and unique childhood, she reflects on a memory of an injured wild owl that she and her siblings saved as children. Surprisingly, when Tara confides her worries to her father, he is sympathetic and suggests that he will help her. Through a chance conversation with a classmate, Tara learns that she is expected to read the textbooks for her classes. Once she starts doing so, her grades improve dramatically.

Analysis: Chapters 15–18

Faye's support for Tara shows that her loyalty and values may be more complex than they initially seem. For much of Tara's childhood, Faye has seemed to embody the life Tara is resistant to living. She tends to appear docile and obedient to her husband and his religious doctrine. It is therefore surprising that when Tara indicates that she might give up on her dream of going to college, Faye is insistent that her daughter should go. Perhaps because of her own life experiences, Faye knows the value of a woman having skills and autonomy. Midwifery and herbalism have given Faye the ability to have some authority and independence, and she wants the same for her daughter. By encouraging Tara not to give up her dream just because she is experiencing setbacks, Faye shows that she is also an ally on Tara's road to independence. Faye's decision to be supportive of Tara's dreams is interesting, given that she has never openly supported her daughter when Gene was critical of Tara's dreams. Faye is very committed to the idea of appearing to be an obedient and subservient wife, so she won't openly contradict her husband. In private, however, she will share her true opinions and her true self with her daughter.

Ironically, Tara reveals her newfound independence by helping the man who is abusing her. Despite everything Shawn has done to her, Tara is horrified when she realizes that her brother has been seriously injured. Her initial impulse to phone their father shows that Tara is still partially an obedient daughter, but her next action shocks both her father and herself. Because Tara already has a plan in place for leaving home and entering the wider world, she is emboldened to defy her father for the first time. Tara also acts out of desperation: she has seen what happened to Shawn when he first suffered brain injuries, so it seems particularly important to secure medical treatment now. Her father's lack of reaction is partially an admission of defeat and acceptance: if Tara is willing to deliberately disobey his explicit instructions, Gene knows that he can never fully control her. Tara is already starting to make her own decisions and act according to her own values. Her education becomes possible when she decides she is going to live life on her own terms.

Tara's initial experiences at college show that she is both intellectually and socially unprepared for higher education. The ACT test relied on skills without context, but much of the college experience relies on assumptions that students know things that Tara is totally ignorant about. Her lack of academic knowledge is almost less of a problem than her lack of study skills and her lack of familiarity with social norms. The experience is even more challenging because Tara isolates herself and refuses to ask for help. Tara is ashamed of being different, and she's also defiantly stubborn about not compromising her values. For these reasons, she doesn't form relationships with new people easily at college, and this makes the adjustment even harder for her.

Even though she struggles when she begins college, Tara shows her resilience and resourcefulness. Her question about the Holocaust is humiliating, but Tara shows her bravery by imitating the behavior of other students and trying to ask a question in class. Even when she is frustrated by her classes, she doesn't drop out. She is willing to do whatever it takes to finance her education, even though she knows that she is facing almost insurmountable obstacles. Perhaps most importantly, Tara has the capacity to learn once she finds the tools that will allow her to do so effectively. As soon as she realizes that reading the textbook is a vital step in the learning process, Tara uses this new information to perform better. Because she is so underprepared, Tara experiences a kind of parallel education alongside her college courses: she learns the class content, and she also learns *how* to learn it.

Chapters 19–22

Summary: Chapter 19

When the semester ends, Tara returns home for the summer. She does not yet know whether she will be able to go back to college in the fall; her grades need to be good enough to earn her a scholarship. Tara wants to work at the local grocery store again to earn money, but her father insists that she join him in the scrapping business. Faced with the threat that she will not be able to live at home unless she goes back to scrapping, Tara quits her job at the grocery store.

Tara's old friend Charles takes an interest in her and asks her out on a date. Shyly, Tara begins to spend more and more time with him. She is also delighted to learn that she has been awarded a scholarship and can return to college in the fall. Although Tara has hoped that Charles will make a romantic gesture, she panics the first time he tries to touch her.

Summary: Chapter 20

Tara's education and new worldliness, as well as her budding relationship with Charles, attract the attention of Shawn and her father. Both men are determined to put Tara in her place. Tara finds the experience of interacting with her father and brother uncomfortable in light of her newly acquired knowledge. For example, her brother uses a racial epithet as a nickname for her. This has not bothered Tara in the past, but she now knows about the history of slavery and the civil rights movement. She understands how wrong it is for her brother to use this term, but she is also powerless to stop him.

Summary: Chapter 21

Shortly before Tara is supposed to go back to college, she develops a severe earache. None of her mother's herbal remedies provide any relief, and when she mentions her pain to Charles, he offers her pain medication. After hesitantly taking the medication, Tara is shocked that her pain disappears.

Tara returns to school, moving in with her new roommates, Robin, Megan, and Jenni. Robin helps Tara learn about some of the social norms she has not previously understood. Tara struggles with her algebra class, and the stress leads her to develop stomach ulcers. Despite the pain, Tara refuses to see a doctor and takes on additional work as a janitor. She is going home to Buck's Peak for Thanksgiving, and she asks Charles if he will help her study algebra during that time.

Summary: Chapter 22

Tara returns home and is nervous about having Charles come to dinner. When Shawn taunts her, the two of them end up in a physical struggle. Once Charles arrives, Shawn attacks Tara again. She is panicked and desperate to prevent Charles from seeing her abuse. Charles rushes out of the house, but he and Tara meet up later that night. She tells him that everything is fine. Driven by shame, Tara and Charles eventually break up.

Back at college, Tara's physical symptoms draw the attention of her roommate Robin. Tara still refuses to see a doctor, and she ignores Robin's suggestion of meeting with a counselor. Tara manages to score a perfect grade on her algebra final, and this result convinces her that she is invincible. Tara returns home for Christmas, observing her brother Richard and noting his intelligence. Tara is shocked when Tyler mentions to her that Gene is supportive of Richard going to college, and eventually learns that her father wants Richard to go to college because he believes that his son will use his intelligence to undermine current cultural values.

Throughout Tara's time at home, Shawn forces her to go into the store where Charles is working while she is wearing her dirty work clothes. When Tara resists, Shawn physically attacks her in the parking lot. That night, Shawn apologizes, and Tara wrestles with confusion about whether she might have misunderstood the events.

Analysis: Chapters 19–22

Tara's relationship with Charles reflects a new stage of emotional development but also shows the lingering trauma of her childhood. Charles may have always had feelings for her, or his attraction may be ignited by seeing Tara as a new person once she has started to build a new life for herself. Tara is acquiring an intellectual education at college, but the possibility of a romantic relationship gives her the chance to learn about herself in a romantic and sexual context. In the same way that she was curious about college and the wider world, Tara is curious about exploring what it means to date Charles. However, even a simple touch from Charles is too much for Tara because she has been taught that her body and her desires are bad and sinful. While she is developing her independence in crucial ways, Tara's panic shows that she is still deeply influenced by the way she was raised.

Along with her intelligence, Tara's grit and resilience become a huge factor in the success of her education. She is capable of excelling in her classes, but she also needs money, and this means that she needs to juggle her classes and work multiple jobs. Because she is used to hard, manual labor, Tara is prepared to do whatever it takes—including taking on a janitorial role—and doesn't even comment on the work she does in her memoir. On top of her many exhausting commitments, Tara must grapple with physical suffering. Her ulcers and tooth problems result directly from her stressful life and an upbringing in which she did not receive proper medical or dental care. Most college students would not have to contend with these problems, but Tara meets her challenges head-on.

Shawn's abusive behavior becomes heightened because he senses that Tara is slipping beyond his control. His sister is now physically absent for months at a time, and she is building a future for herself where she will someday be able to live and work independently from the family, if she chooses. Tara's relationship with Charles also shows Shawn that she is starting to make her own choices, and that she is drawn to a man who is not seeking to control or dominate her. Shawn's physical abuse becomes more pronounced and blatant, and he does not care whether people outside of the family know what is happening. Shawn is also psychologically astute, and knows how to cause Tara shame, which hurts her more than any of the physical abuse does.

Despite her increasing independence, Tara still second-guesses the severity of what Shawn is doing and blames herself. When Tara realizes that Charles has seen the way Shawn treats her, she reacts with intense shame, as if *she* were the one who had done something wrong. Tara is terrified of pity. In her family, vulnerability is wielded against people, so she cannot imagine Charles feeling compassion for her. Because of the abuse, Tara's view of the world becomes very distorted, and she isolates herself. Her shame and insecurity allow Shawn to prey on her further, because Tara is always tempted to blame herself or minimize what has happened. Shawn does seem to sometimes experience genuine regret, even though he always repeats his abusive behavior later on. Because Tara is not confident in her own perspective, she can fall victim to believing that nothing bad is happening to her.

Chapters 23–25

Summary: Chapter 23

Tara is asked out on dates by several men in her church congregation, but she turns them down. As a result, she is called into a meeting with the bishop. Noticing that something is wrong, the bishop asks Tara to keep meeting with him. To her surprise, she starts to talk openly with him about her life and her family.

When the semester ends, Tara needs to go home and work. The bishop recommends that she stay away, offering to give her money for her rent, but Tara insists on returning home. The bishop does get her to promise that she will not work for her father, so Tara returns to working at the grocery store instead. As a result, she heads back to school with much less money than she needs. Two weeks into the semester, she comes down with severe tooth pain that requires expensive dental work. Her parents offer to lend her the money on the condition that she work for them next summer, and she refuses to do so. Tara tries to ignore the pain.

Learning about the suffering Tara endures, the bishop suggests that she apply for a grant or take money from the church, but she refuses to do either. Tara spends a desperate semester barely scraping by, and by Christmas break, she has no money left. She plans to move to Las Vegas to live with her brother Tony. Then, Shawn surprises Tara by giving her just enough money to return to school in January. Still, Tara can barely pay her bills, even with a second job, and the bishop keeps urging her to apply for a grant. Finally, Tara submits the application. She receives a grant and, for the first time, feels financially secure. She also knows that she will not need to work for her father ever again.

Summary: Chapter 24

With her financial problems resolved, Tara focuses on her studies again. Based on a lecture in her psychology class, she begins to suspect that her father is mentally ill. This idea also leads her to research the shooting of the Weaver family at Ruby Ridge. Her father has always told her this story in the context of a family having been mercilessly killed by federal agents after refusing to send their children to school. Tara learns that while family members, including children, were killed, the conflict was triggered by Weaver's involvement in white nationalist movements. Her father's paranoid delusions caused him to completely misinterpret events.

Tara begins to research and write about bipolar disorder. She becomes much angrier, and eventually confronts her father about the way his behavior has impacted her life. She stays in Utah for the summer. She moves to an apartment, interns at a law firm, and starts dating a man named Nick. When she falls ill, Nick insists that she see a doctor. Tara is prescribed antibiotics and tells her mother, who is disappointed with her for turning to scientific medicine. The next morning, Audrey calls to tell Tara that their father has been in a serious accident.

Summary: Chapter 25

Tara reflects on a family story. When her grandfather was seriously injured while working alone on the mountain, angels came to help him and saved his life. Her father has been injured in an accident where a fuel tanker exploded and has suffered severe burns to his face and fingers. Tara goes to Idaho, horrified by her father's condition. Against all odds, Gene slowly begins to recover.

Analysis: Chapters 23–25

The bishop is the first person whom Tara truly trusts and opens herself up to. Because he is an authority figure, Tara is obedient enough to keep meeting with him, even though she initially has no desire to tell him anything. Tara does not include many details about the bishop's reaction to her stories, but it is clear that he is a non-judgmental presence. Rather than blaming Tara, he does everything he can to help her. Even more than the practical support he offers, his reaction is vital to allowing Tara to trust others and build relationships for herself. She has always feared that if she tells anyone the truth about her past and her family, they will turn against her. Instead, the bishop's reaction shows Tara that people can show her compassion and offer help.

Financial support becomes increasingly crucial to Tara's education; hard work and determination alone are not enough to ensure success. Tara is very intellectually gifted, and she does everything in her power to afford her education. Nonetheless, she comes close to hitting rock-bottom several times. Shawn and the bishop help her secure the money she needs to continue her education. The money from Shawn, even though it is a small amount, is emotionally complex in the context of their abusive relationship. The money from the grant should feel more straightforward, but Tara actually feels more shame about applying for a government grant. Nonetheless, the money Tara receives liberates her, allowing her to fully devote her attention to her studies. This change is reflected in Tara's interest and academic performance, which shows how adequate finances are crucial to academic success for any student.

The knowledge Tara gains makes her increasingly skeptical and angry about the way she has been forced to live her life. Tara realizes that she has been denied accurate information about how the world works, especially after discovering mental illness, the true nature of what happened at the Weaver shoot-out, and the effectiveness of painkillers. Her ideas and beliefs have all been formed through a distorted lens, and now she needs to reconsider them. Tara is finally independent enough to look at the way her family raised her and see that she has been mistreated and denied opportunities that most other children had. This anger fuels her to push away from her family.

Gene's terrible burns reflect the tragic nature of his life. Faye is sufficiently terrified by her husband's injury that she is willing to seek medical aid, but Gene's beliefs are so ingrained that he refuses. The fact that he hangs on to his beliefs even amid agonizing physical pain—and the very real possibility that he might die—shows just how warped his worldview is. Gene's pain is important because it evokes pity for him from Tara and from the reader. At this point, he seems more and more like a villain because of the childhood he has imposed on Tara and his other children. The way he suffers due to his mental illness and paranoia shows that he is also a victim of his own fate.

Chapters 26–29

Summary: Chapter 26

Gene spends two months in bed, nursed by Tara, her mother, and some of her siblings. His weakened condition means that Tara begins to tell him about her life, hopeful that they might enter into a new stage of their relationship. Meanwhile, Shawn announces that he is engaged to a woman named Emily. Tara is convinced that Shawn is already being abusive toward her and will only get worse, so she seeks out a chance to speak with Emily alone. To Tara's surprise, Emily confides that she is frightened of Shawn and his abuse, but also believes that he has a spiritual mission.

When Tara returns to Utah, she considers telling Nick the truth about everything, but she is still too ashamed. She hides the truth about her family from him. In September, Emily and Shawn get married, and Tara breaks up with Nick, because she doesn't believe she will ever be able to be honest with him.

Summary: Chapter 27

In her junior year, Tara switches from studying music to history. Tara confides in her history professor, telling him about her unconventional schooling. He suggests that she consider applying to a study-abroad program at the University of Cambridge in England.

When Tara returns to Buck's Peak for Christmas, her father is treated as a hero and prophet for surviving his terrible accident. Meanwhile, Emily struggles with a difficult pregnancy. In the winter semester, Tara learns that her Cambridge application has been rejected, but her professor has intervened on her behalf and she has been accepted. In February, Emily gives birth to a tiny, premature baby at home in a snowstorm and has to be rushed to the hospital. Miraculously, both Emily and the baby survive, but the events make Tara further question her family's reliance on trusting God.

Summary: Chapter 28

> *Dad could be wrong, and the great historians Carlyle and Macaulay and Trevelyn could be wrong, but from the ashes of their dispute I could construct a world to live in. In knowing the ground was not ground at all, I hoped I could stand on it.*
>
> *(See* QUOTATIONS, *p. 49)*

Tara is astonished by the world she encounters when she arrives at Cambridge for her study-abroad program. She plans to work on a research project with Professor Steinberg, who is fascinated by Tara's story of her unconventional educational background. Under his guidance, Tara reaches a new level of critical analysis and writing.

Professor Steinberg quickly begins to discuss Tara's plans for graduate school, suggesting that she might study at Cambridge and assuring her he that will handle the financial details. Noticing her discomfort, he urges her to believe in herself, but Tara is still fixated on her shame.

Summary: Chapter 29

After Tara returns to BYU, she plans to forget about Cambridge, but Professor Steinberg urges her to apply for the Gates Cambridge Scholarship, which could potentially fund her graduate studies. By February, Tara has been awarded the Gates Scholarship. When interviewed by the press about winning the scholarship, she never mentions having been homeschooled, and her father tells her that he is disappointed in her for hiding her upbringing. Nonetheless, her parents do attend her graduation, and drive her to the airport on the night she flies to England.

Analysis: Chapters 26–29

Emily embodies how other young women also suffer abuse and oppression within the world of Tara's family. Tara has watched Shawn abuse every woman he has ever dated, so she has no doubt that he will abuse his wife as well. Tara's determination to save Emily from a lifetime of suffering shows that she has seen enough of the world to know that what happens on Buck's Peak is wrong. Even though Tara has found it impossible to stand up for herself, she finds the strength to intervene for Emily by warning her. Emily, however, has not developed the critical thinking and strength that Tara has. Emily would rather submit to Shawn's beatings than challenge his claims of holiness. The true damage that has been inflicted on Emily is not just the physical abuse she receives, but the way she has accepted it. Emily represents what might have happened to Tara if she had not found a life outside of the family home. When Faye delivers Emily's baby under dangerous conditions, it also becomes clear that the entire system of tradition and expectation is going to render Emily powerless to change her life.

Tara's experience on the study-abroad program at Cambridge pushes her intellectual growth and self-understanding further than she ever could have imagined. College itself was a huge departure, but Cambridge shows her a whole new world where people's entire lives revolve around intellectual pursuits. Despite her desire to drink in as much as she can, Tara also feels totally lost and alienated. Even to herself, she can't fully understand why she always feels like such an outcast. While Tara may struggle with feeling like she doesn't belong, her academic performance indicates otherwise. Tara never explores whether there is any connection between her unconventional upbringing and the quality of the academic work she achieves, but all of the professors she encounters are struck by her.

Tara's decision to attend graduate school tests the limits of how far she can go without breaking from her family completely. Even changing her major from music to history was a big decision because it signaled that she was becoming more engaged in intellectual work that might lead her to question and challenge the doctrines she has grown up with. Tara's decision to go to graduate school is even more radical because it means that she will be geographically far away from her family and building networks of relationships totally separate from them. Gene fears that he will not be able to get to Tara if an apocalyptic event takes place. By this point, it is becoming more and more clear that Tara is building a life that will be dramatically different from the one her parents once expected her to lead.

Chapters 30–33

Summary: Chapter 30

> *Never had I found such comfort in a void, in the black absence of knowledge. It seemed to say: whatever you are, you are woman.*
>
> (*See* QUOTATIONS, *p. 50*)

Tara moves into her new dormitory at Cambridge and attends classes. Tara finally has the revelation that she has not fully committed to living in the modern, educated world she has chosen, and starts to take steps. One thing she does is get her vaccinations. Tara also becomes interested in feminism, and realizes that she is not alone in questioning the doctrine of feminine obedience.

When Tara goes back to America for Christmas, she is pleased to see her brother Richard, who is studying chemistry, with his wife and young son. The holiday seems peaceful enough, until one freezing night, when Emily comes rushing into the family home. Shawn has thrown her into a snowbank and locked her outside barefoot and wearing only light clothing. Tara urges Richard and his wife not to interfere, and to leave the situation to her father. Gene eventually gets Shawn to come to the house and lectures his son about his behavior. Shawn leaves with Emily, and Tara regrets that she didn't stand up for her sister-in-law.

Summary: Chapter 31

> *I didn't understand the magic of those words then, and I don't understand it now. I know only this: that when my mother told me she had not been the mother to me that she wished she had been, she became that mother for the first time.*
>
> *(See* QUOTATIONS, *p. 50)*

Before Tara goes back to England, she visits Audrey. Audrey is homeschooling her children, and Tara worries about the fate of her nieces and nephews. Back at Cambridge, Tara eagerly immerses herself in academic life again. She excels in her academic work and is encouraged to consider pursuing a PhD. Over spring break, she travels to Rome with some classmates. The city helps Tara connect to the past and to her work as a historian.

When Tara returns from Rome, she gets an email from Audrey. Audrey confides that Shawn abused her as well, and that Audrey has always blamed herself for not helping Tara. Now, Audrey is going to confront Shawn and their parents, and she wants Tara to help her and share her story as well. Tara replies, agreeing with Audrey, but asks Audrey to wait until she gets back to Idaho before taking any action. However, Audrey shows Faye the email from Tara as confirmation of Shawn's behavior and Faye reaches out to Tara online, indicating that she believes her daughter and blames herself for having lived in ignorance for so long. Faye also admits that Gene suffers from bipolar disorder. Tara leaves the conversation feeling relieved and supported.

A week later, Tara hears from her mother that Gene knows about what Shawn has done, and that he is going to get help. Tara feels hopeful about the future for her family, and she begins to be much more transparent about her past with her new friends and colleagues at Cambridge.

Summary: Chapter 32

Tara returns to Buck's Peak to see her dying grandmother. Her parents' business is thriving, but after the death of his mother, Gene lapses into depression. Tara notices that her mother is being more assertive, but that the relationship between her parents seems to be deteriorating.

Summary: Chapter 33

Before Tara leaves, Audrey asks her to stay and help her confront Shawn, but Tara refuses. By now, Tara is in a relationship with a man named Drew, who is also studying at Cambridge. She is immersed in her doctoral research, which will focus on the connection between Mormon theology and other intellectual traditions, and she is happy with her close circle of friends. Feeling ashamed at her lack of connection to Idaho, Tara forces herself to spend Christmas with her family. While in Idaho, Shawn confronts Tara and tells her that Audrey is spreading lies.

Analysis: Chapters 30–33

Although Tara seems to be building an independent life, revelations from Emily and Audrey pull her back into the drama of her abusive family. Her English life creates a radically new dynamic between Tara and her family, but Tara has always felt concerned about the fate Emily would suffer while married to Shawn, so she is horrified by the graphic confirmation of Emily's abuse, and even more so by the knowledge that her parents are unwilling to intervene in any meaningful way. Tara is filled with regret and shame at her inability to do more to help Emily, and she therefore reacts even more strongly to Audrey's confession that she was also abused by Shawn. Tara has felt so alone in her shame that it is a revelation to learn that other women have had similar experiences.

Faye's apology and promise of support transform Tara's concept of self-worth. Faye's reaction is long delayed and doesn't promise much about what will happen in the future, but it still fills Tara with peace and hope. Tara has always longed for her mother to protect and nurture her. Now, at last, Faye shows love and compassion to Tara, and Tara forgives her wholeheartedly. Despite all the abuse and betrayal she has suffered, Tara is not embittered toward her family. If anything, she trusts them too easily, since she rushes to accept Faye's apology without making Faye do anything to earn her trust and show that she has changed the way she intends to behave. Aside from the way it changes her relationship with her family, Faye's apology lifts Tara's shame for the first time in her life. Tara has always felt the lingering fear that perhaps the abuse was all her own fault, or that she was imagining everything. Now, Tara can truly know that she hasn't done anything wrong and doesn't have anything to feel ashamed of.

Paradoxically, Tara's independence and stability sometimes seem to drive her back toward her family. The more her life in England seems to be thriving, the more Tara feels compelled to maintain her ties with Buck's Peak. In comparison with the fate of young women like Audrey and Emily, Tara likely feels guilty that she can travel the world, study, and essentially be free to do whatever she wants. Tara also knows that she has less and less in common with her family members as her life moves steadily in a different direction. While this knowledge might seem liberating, it also terrifies her. Despite everything, Tara does not want to lose contact with her family, and she is always afraid they will cast her off. They are still the only people who truly know everything about her, and Tara is unwilling to let the relationship slip away completely.

Because he can no longer control Tara, Shawn becomes obsessed with controlling the narrative about his behavior. One way Shawn asserts his control over his victims is to gaslight them, or make them disbelieve their own stories. Getting his victims to be complicit and accepting of whatever happens to them gives Shawn the ultimate power thrill. When Audrey speaks out about Shawn's abuse, his power is undermined. Shawn is willing to threaten extreme violence if it allows him to regain a sense of control. Tara has to exercise extreme caution in the face of his anger, and this dynamic reduces her back to being at the mercy of her brother's anger.

Chapters 34–36

Summary: Chapter 34

When she gets home, Tara tells her father that Shawn has threatened Audrey, and that she suspects Audrey has confronted Shawn about his abusive past. Gene is unwilling to accept Tara's statements about Shawn without proof. Tara expects her mother to take her side, but she's horrified when she realizes that Faye is not going to stand up for her. Tara flees in tears and comes back to learn that her father has told Shawn to come to the house.

When Shawn arrives, he threatens Tara and hands her a bloody knife. Tara has a disembodied experience wherein she renounces her claims, insisting that she has never accused Shawn of anything. Gene's droning lecture focuses on the need for feminine obedience, and Shawn leaves calmly, feeling justified. After Shawn leaves, Tara phones Drew, who urges her to leave. So as not to disrupt the fragile calm, Tara waits until the morning, and then drives away. Passing her brother's trailer, she sees blood in the snow outside. She will later learn that after Shawn received the phone call from their father, he killed his pet dog with a knife.

Looking back on the traumatic events, Tara understands that, despite the online conversation with her mother, Faye had never spoken with Gene or confronted Shawn.

Summary: Chapter 35

> *Everything I had worked for, all my years of study, had been to purchase for myself this one privilege: to see and experience more truths than those given to me by my father, and to use those truths to construct my own mind.*
>
> *(See* QUOTATIONS, *p. 51)*

Tara returns to Cambridge and waits in fear for the confrontation when Shawn will come to understand that she had deliberately told her parents about what he did to her. In early March, Shawn reaches out to her and threatens her life. Tara tells her parents what is happening, but they do little to help her. Eventually, Shawn cuts Tara out of his life entirely. Her mother also disagrees with the account of what happened the night of the confrontation.

That summer, Tara goes to Paris with Drew. While there, she receives an email from Audrey. Audrey tells her that their father is insisting that Tara and Audrey forgive Shawn. Audrey has decided to forgive Shawn, and now she blames Tara for having corrupted her and given her evil ideas. She is cutting ties with Tara as well. Tara realizes that her relationship with her family is likely damaged beyond repair. She also, however, begins to question her own memory and even her own sanity. Desperate, Tara contacts Erin, a woman whom Shawn used to date. Erin confirms that everything Tara claims also happened to her.

Tara never fully feels certain of her memories until years later when she runs into a man in Utah who recognizes her last name and mentions Shawn. He says that he witnessed Shawn assaulting a young woman, and Tara takes this as confirmation that everything she remembers about Shawn is true.

Summary: Chapter 36

Tara arrives at Harvard and begins her studies there. She is shocked to learn that her parents are going to visit her in Boston. Shortly before the visit, Tara gets in contact with Charles, who suggests that Tara should just sever ties with her family. Tara's parents are desperate to convert her back to the faith, and she wishes she could just fall back on her old beliefs.

Tara travels with her parents to visit several important Mormon sites, and her father tells her that she has fallen prey to Satan. Tara goes with her parents to Niagara Falls and has a moment of happiness with them. Before her parents leave, her father offers to give her a blessing. Tara refuses. Her father predicts that she is going to suffer and will need the support of God and her family. Still, Tara stands her ground. Her parents leave almost immediately afterward.

Analysis: Chapters 34–36

Tara's attempt to reveal what Shawn has done to her ends with her being betrayed by the female family members in whom she placed her trust. When Tara's mother first told her that she believes Tara's account of the abuse and will intervene, Tara did not hesitate to trust Faye. This innocent faith makes the crushing betrayal of learning that Faye did nothing—and will not defend Tara—so much worse. Tara has always feared abandonment and having her family turn their back on her, and now this fear comes to pass. First her mother, and then Audrey, decide that it is more important to preserve their relationships with Gene and Shawn. These women do not have access to the same independence that Tara does, and they fear the unknown. Tara becomes the scapegoat.

The lack of familial support creates additional trauma by making Tara question her sanity. With the very real fear that Shawn might attack and kill her, Tara makes a choice of self-preservation, and pretends that she never accused Shawn of abuse. While this action keeps her physically safe, it takes a huge psychological toll, since Tara effectively betrays herself. The decision is even more traumatic because everyone around Tara accuses her of either lying or being delusional, and she goes along with these claims. Tara is in very real danger of losing her own conviction in her sanity, and giving in to the idea that nothing has happened to her, and that she has just been overreacting all along.

Shawn's violence and anger confirm that there is no hope of resurrecting a relationship with him. Shawn has shown moments of possibly having some lingering kindness and humanity, but once Tara starts to talk openly about the abuse, his rage is too far gone. Shawn is determined to protect his reputation and his relationship with the family at all costs. He is prepared to drive Tara away, or worse. Although Tara has suffered so much, she has never been willing to cut Shawn out of her life, and knowing that her brother will always hate and despise her is excruciating. Tara hoped that speaking the truth would somehow heal her family, but in the short term, it seems only to cost her.

Knowing that her family has completely failed to protect and nurture her, Tara finally finds the courage to fully defy them. Tara has gradually been taking steps toward independence, but she has never fully relinquished her relationship with her family. She still treats Buck's Peak like the home she will invariably return to, and she at least maintains outward expectations of loving and honoring her parents. When her parents side with Shawn, Tara realizes they have never done any of the things parents are supposed to do for their children, and this makes her question why she needs to keep behaving like an obedient daughter. While it is painful, this final betrayal gives Tara clarity and freedom. By refusing her father's blessing, Tara draws a boundary for the first time in her adult life. She will never stop loving her parents, but she also needs to live according to her own standards and beliefs.

Chapters 37–40

Summary: Chapter 37

After her parents' visit, Tara lapses into depression. Desperate to reconcile with her family, she books a plane ticket to Buck's Peak. By accident, Tara sees an email from her mother to Erin in which her mother writes that Shawn has been saved, and Tara is under the influence of the devil. Faye also writes about having delivered Emily's second baby, and how she thanks God for helping her with the dangerous delivery. Tara is furious that her mother delivered the baby at home while knowing how dangerous it was going to be. She closes the email and leaves the house.

Tara is planning to fly back to Boston when she gets a call from Tyler. Their mother has reached out to him. Tyler wonders why Tara didn't confide in him sooner. Tara assumes that he would not believe her, but Tyler takes her side immediately. He has had his own experiences with Shawn's violence, and has no reason to mistrust Tara.

After completing her fellowship, Tara travels to the Middle East with Drew. She is in awe of the experiences she has had since leaving home, but also mourns for her relationship with her family. She decides to sever ties with her family for one year in order to heal.

Summary: Chapter 38

Tara's emotional distress leaves her severely behind in her schoolwork, and she fears that she won't be able to complete her PhD. She is still in contact with Tyler, who tries to persuade their parents to be more sympathetic to Tara, but he is not successful. Eventually, Shawn threatens to exile Tyler from the family if he keeps persisting. Tara fears that she is going to lose Tyler as well, convinced that he will choose the "stability" of the family over his relationship with her. Astonished, she receives a letter from Tyler declaring that he supports Tara and views the family as abusive.

Tara starts attending counseling. Eventually, Tara focuses on her academic work again and returns to her research. She submits her dissertation on her twenty-seventh birthday and defends her thesis a few months later.

Summary: Chapter 39

The spring after completing her PhD, Tara returns to Idaho. She visits her grandparents and asks her mother to come and meet her in town. Tara's mother refuses, saying she will not go against the will of her husband, and she will only see Tara if she comes to the house.

When Tara's grandmother dies, she wants to go to Idaho to attend the funeral, but doesn't know where she will stay. She reaches out to her mother's sister Angie and stays with her. At the funeral, Tara watches her siblings gather. Tara, Tyler, and Richard now all have doctorates, and are living independent lives, but her other four siblings and their spouses work for her parents. They are also homeschooling their children.

Summary: Chapter 40

Tara concludes her memoir with an update on her situation. At the time she finishes writing, she has not seen her parents in years. She keeps in contact with Tyler, Richard, and Tony. She has achieved some measure of peace with her relationship with her family, but she does not know if she will ever be in contact with her father again. This journey to independence has cost her greatly, but it has also changed her forever.

Analysis: Chapters 37–40

After suffering so many betrayals, Tara finally receives steadfast loyalty from Tyler. Tyler has always been a strong supporter of Tara. He has also known since Tara was young that Shawn was violent toward her, since this is part of the reason Tyler first encouraged Tara to move away and go to school. Significantly, Tyler is more independent and objective than the other family members who betrayed Tara's trust when she confided in them. Like Tara, Tyler is educated, employed, and has built a new family for himself. For all of these reasons, he can stand up to his family without living in fear of losing everything. Tyler's willingness to openly state his support for Tara makes her feel less alone and abandoned, which helps her to heal. Nonetheless, Tyler does not sever contact with his family, even after he knows what Tara has gone through.

Tara channels her desire for family, love, and support into building a new relationship with her extended family. In the end, even with the new life she has built for herself, Tara still needs a connection to her past and her roots. She has never been close with her mother's family because she was raised to believe they were critical of her father. Now, after everything she has been through, Tara is also critical of her family, and can see why her grandmother and aunts felt the way they did. By building a new relationship with them, Tara shows her resilience and ability to compromise. She may never be able to have a relationship with her immediate family, but she has the freedom and resourcefulness to make choices and seek out love and support wherever she can find it.

When she began her journey toward going to college, Tara could not have imagined how her life would unfold, or the magnitude of the choices she would make. Looking back and connecting the events of her life into a story, she can see how all her actions had interconnected consequences. In some ways, it might have been easier to live in ignorance and blind trust, because she would not have had to think for herself or take responsibility for her choices. Once she became educated, she also became morally responsible for living according to her values and being the kind of woman she can respect. Her education may have given her more questions than answers, but it has also given her the possibility to choose.

Important Quotations Explained

1. *After that night, there was never a question of whether I would go or stay. It was as if we were living in the future, and I was already gone.*

This quotation occurs in Chapter 16, after Tara disobeys her father and takes Shawn to the hospital to be treated for injuries he sustained in a motorcycle accident. This action marks the beginning of a pattern wherein she acts independently of her family and makes choices which contradict the values she grew up with. At this point, Tara has not yet gone away to school, and is still hesitating about whether pursuing an education is the right decision for her. In defying her father, she starts to develop the confidence to take other independent actions. This quote also shows the role of the retrospective narration in the memoir. At the time when Tara made the choice to take Shawn to the hospital, she could not see the full significance and impact of this choice. Looking back, she can see patterns and connections between the different actions that eventually led her away from her family.

2. *Dad could be wrong, and the great historians Carlyle and Macaulay and Trevelyn could be wrong, but from the ashes of their dispute I could construct a world to live in. In knowing the ground was not ground at all, I hoped I could stand on it.*

This quotation occurs in Chapter 28, when Tara is first at Cambridge and announces her plan to study historiography (the study of history and historians). Tara has grown up in a family with clear narratives she is expected to believe in, and her father always presents his beliefs with total certainty. Part of why Tara grows apart from her family and becomes interested in getting an education is that she always has a sense that reality is more complex than her father has taught her.

3. *Never had I found such comfort in a void, in the black absence of knowledge. It seemed to say: whatever you are, you are woman.*

This quotation occurs in Chapter 30, after Tara becomes interested in the history of feminism and reads a quote from John Stuart Mill saying that nothing definitive can be known about the nature of women. Growing up, Tara has often been critical about gender roles and expectations for women. She has been raised to believe that women should not have ambitions, should be obedient to men, and should not question male authority. However, Tara knows from watching her mother, and from her own experiences, that women can be smart, capable, and strong. This contrast has left Tara feeling confused and ashamed. She thinks there must be something wrong with her because she cannot reconcile what she has been told about women with how she actually feels about being a woman. This confusion is what drives her to finally become curious about what thinkers and writers from the past have had to say about this subject. Tara finds the quotation from Mill comforting because it gives her space for self-definition and creating her own identity.

4. *I didn't understand the magic of those words then, and I don't understand it now. I know only this: that when my mother told me she had not been the mother to me that she wished she had been, she became that mother for the first time.*

This quotation occurs in Chapter 31, after Tara's mother apologizes for failing to protect her daughter from Shawn. Tara is moved by Faye's apology and feels truly loved for the first time. This is a moment when Tara feels a sense of hope about the future relationship she might someday have with her family. Her mother's apology makes it seem possible that they are starting a new chapter, and that things are going to be different in the future. It also represents a new dynamic because in Tara's family, the parents are usually unquestioned figures of authority. This quotation represents the first time one of her parents admits that they have made a mistake and have regrets.

5. *Everything I had worked for, all my years of study, had been to purchase for myself this one privilege: to see and experience more truths than those given to me by my father, and to use those truths to construct my own mind.*

This quotation occurs in Chapter 36, when Tara hesitates over whether to let her father give her a blessing, before ultimately refusing. This refusal represents a definitive turning point in their relationship, and the end of the possibility that Tara will ever be submissive to her father again. If Tara accepts his blessing, she is indicating that she still follows his religious faith and relies on him to direct her with his authority. Tara realizes that she has made many sacrifices in order to pursue her education. More than anything, her education has given her the ability to think for herself. She is no longer a naïve child who sees her father as the ultimate authority figure. She knows that there are many perspectives on how to view the world, and she wants to be free to choose for herself. Tara's education has set her free, but it has also made it impossible for her to blindly submit to her father's authority. This quotation represents a moment of empowerment for Tara, but also a moment of sadness. Tara's father has no other framework to guide his relationship with his daughter. If he cannot dominate and control her, he will choose to not have a relationship with her at all.

Key Facts

FULL TITLE
Educated

AUTHOR
Tara Westover

TYPE OF WORK
Memoir

GENRE
Coming-of-age

LANGUAGE
English

TIME AND PLACE WRITTEN
England and America; 2016–2018

DATE OF FIRST PUBLICATION
2018

PUBLISHER
Penguin Random House

NARRATOR
Tara Westover narrates the memoir retrospectively, looking back at events from her childhood and young adulthood.

POINT OF VIEW
Tara narrates the memoir in the first person, describing events according to what she has seen and heard. Tara gives readers access to her inner thoughts and motivations. Tara also acknowledges that she is presenting events and conversations according to what she remembers, and that those memories might be unreliable. At times, she describes an event from her point of view, and then also includes the same event according to what a different character remembers.

TONE
Regretful; ambivalent; defiant; triumphant

TENSE

Most of the memoir is told in the past tense, since Tara is looking back at events from her earlier life. She occasionally uses the present tense to reflect on the feelings and ideas that surface as she writes her memoir.

SETTING (TIME)

1996–2014

SETTING (PLACE)

Idaho, Utah, England

PROTAGONIST

Tara Westover

MAJOR CONFLICT

Tara struggles to break free from her controlling and violent family who want her to live a life of isolation and obedience.

RISING ACTION

Tara becomes increasingly curious about the wider world, and eventually goes to college and graduate school, where she realizes that she wants to think for herself and make her own decisions.

CLIMAX

Tara refuses to let her father give her a traditional Mormon blessing, showing that she will no longer adhere to the religion or follow his authority, and that she is always going to value her own free will more than her relationship with her family.

FALLING ACTION

Tara makes several efforts to continue to have a relationship with her family, but gradually realizes that her parents and most of her siblings will not have a relationship with her unless she becomes more submissive and reconciles with her father.

THEMES

The power of knowledge; the instability of memory; conflict between identities

MOTIFS

Injuries; the mountain

SYMBOLS

Penicillin; Caravaggio's *Judith Beheading Holofernes*; the bloody knife

FORESHADOWING

Luke's burns foreshadow the burns Tara's father will suffer; Emily's refusal to listen to warnings that Shawn is abusive foreshadow the refusal of Tara's parents to believe their son is abusive; Faye's estrangement from her family foreshadows Tara's estrangement

Study Questions

1. *What role does Tara's extended family play in her independence?*

Because Tara leads a very isolated childhood, her extended family represents almost the only people she knows outside of her parents and siblings. Because of this dynamic, Tara's grandparents and aunts are among the first people who show her that it is possible to criticize and challenge her father's authority. In different ways, both her maternal and paternal grandmothers are critical of the way Gene leads his life and raises his family. Her paternal grandmother even offers to kidnap Tara and take her to another state where she can attend school, while her maternal grandmother shows her an alternative set of values. As a child, Tara is too young to fully understand what all of this means, but it does leave her with the impression that there might be ways of seeing the world that are different from her father's point of view. Her grandparents will also applaud her decision to go to college, while her own father disapproves of it. Later, Tara's aunts and grandmother help her establish independence by offering her an alternative family support system. When Tara eventually becomes estranged from her parents and most of her siblings, her extended family loves and accepts Tara for who she is and does not ask her to change.

2. *Why does Tara find it difficult to pursue romantic relationships?*

There are two primary reasons that Tara finds it difficult to pursue romantic relationships. First, she reacts with shame and disgust whenever a man tries to show her physical affection. When Tara first returns home from college and starts dating Charles, she is curious and attracted to him. However, when Charles tries to touch her, she panics. Her family has made her feel that her body is shameful and sinful, and Tara becomes overwhelmed at the thought of being close with someone. In particular, Shawn has taunted her about the relationship and has always made Tara feel ashamed of herself.

Secondly, Tara tries to hide her history and her family from anyone she dates, and this makes it impossible to achieve true intimacy. Tara is ashamed of her family, and the abuse she is subjected to, and she assumes that if she ever confides in anyone she is dating, he will be repelled by it. As a result, she is always carrying around a shameful secret and her partners get frustrated that she won't trust and confide in them. First Charles and then Nick are driven away by Tara's inability to be vulnerable and open with them. Once Drew becomes a steady presence in Tara's life, she has much more confidence to break from her family and not be afraid of being cast out.

3. *What role do Shawn's girlfriends and wife play in the memoir?*

Shawn displays a consistent pattern of abuse toward every woman he has intimate interactions with. He abuses his girlfriends, Sadie and Erin, and then his wife Emily. He also abuses both of his sisters during the years they live at home as teenagers. Shawn's girlfriends and wife inspire Tara to stand up to Shawn and also to believe in herself. Because Tara often second-guesses herself and doubts whether or not Shawn is actually abusing her, these other women play a key role in helping her have faith in her own convictions. When Tara is desperate to have someone confirm Shawn's abusive behavior, she reaches out to Erin, who agrees with everything Tara says and confirms that Shawn also hurt her. When Tara also witnesses Emily being abused after Shawn throws her into a snowbank on a freezing-cold night, Tara realizes that she has not been imagining things, and that Shawn is capable of terrible violence. These confirmations are very important because so many other characters betray Tara and gaslight her. Even if she does not have close relationships with these women, they give her a reassuring sense of her own sanity, which builds her confidence to tell her story.

How to Write Literary Analysis

The Literary Essay: A Step-by-Step Guide

When you read for pleasure, your only goal is enjoyment. You might find yourself reading to get caught up in an exciting story, to learn about an interesting time or place, or just to pass time. Maybe you're looking for inspiration, guidance, or a reflection of your own life. There are as many different, valid ways of reading a book as there are books in the world.

When you read a work of literature in an English class, however, you're being asked to read in a special way: you're being asked to perform *literary analysis*. To analyze something means to break it down into smaller parts and then examine how those parts work, both individually and together. Literary analysis involves examining all the parts of a novel, play, short story, or poem—elements such as character, setting, tone, and imagery—and thinking about how the author uses those elements to create certain effects.

A literary essay isn't a book review: you're not being asked whether or not you liked a book or whether you'd recommend it to another reader. A literary essay also isn't like the kind of book report you wrote when you were younger, when your teacher wanted you to summarize the book's action. A high school or college–level literary essay asks, "How does this piece of literature actually work?" "How does it do what it does?" and, "Why might the author have made the choices he or she did?"

The Seven Steps

No one is born knowing how to analyze literature; it's a skill and a process you can master. As you gain more practice with this kind of thinking and writing, you'll be able to craft a method that works best for you. But until then, here are seven basic steps to writing a well-constructed literary essay:

1. *Ask questions*
2. *Collect evidence*
3. *Construct a thesis*

4. *Develop and organize arguments*
5. *Write the introduction*
6. *Write the body paragraphs*
7. *Write the conclusion*

---

1. Ask Questions

When you're assigned a literary essay in class, your teacher will often provide you with a list of writing prompts. Lucky you! Now all you have to do is choose one. Do yourself a favor and pick a topic that interests you. You'll have a much better (not to mention easier) time if you start off with something you enjoy thinking about. If you are asked to come up with a topic by yourself, though, you might start to feel a little panicked. Maybe you have too many ideas—or none at all. Don't worry. Take a deep breath and start by asking yourself these questions:

- **What struck you?** Did a particular image, line, or scene linger in your mind for a long time? If it fascinated you, chances are you can draw on it to write a fascinating essay.
- **What confused you?** Maybe you were surprised to see a character act in a certain way, or maybe you didn't understand why the book ended the way it did. Confusing moments in a work of literature are like a loose thread in a sweater: if you pull on it, you can unravel the entire thing. Ask yourself why the author chose to write about that character or scene the way he or she did, and you might tap into some important insights about the work as a whole.
- **Did you notice any patterns?** Is there a phrase that the main character uses constantly or an image that repeats throughout the book? If you can figure out how that pattern weaves through the work and what the significance of that pattern is, you've almost got your entire essay mapped out.
- **Did you notice any contradictions or ironies?** Great works of literature are complex; great literary essays recognize and explain those complexities. Maybe the title of the work seems to contradict its content (for example, the play *Happy Days* shows its two characters buried up to their waists in dirt). Maybe the main character acts one way around his or her family and a completely different way around his or her friends and associates. If you can find a way to explain

a work's contradictory elements, you've got the seeds of a great essay.

At this point, you don't need to know exactly what you're going to say about your topic; you just need a place to begin your exploration. You can help direct your reading and brainstorming by formulating your topic as a *question*, which you'll then try to answer in your essay. The best questions invite critical debates and discussions, not just a rehashing of the summary. Remember, you're looking for something you can *prove or argue* based on evidence you find in the text. Finally, remember to keep the scope of your question in mind: is this a topic you can adequately address within the word or page limit you've been given? Conversely, is this a topic big enough to fill the required length?

GOOD QUESTIONS

"Are Romeo and Juliet's parents responsible for the deaths of their children?"

"Why do pigs keep showing up in Lord of the Flies*?"*

"Are Dr. Frankenstein and his monster alike? How?"

BAD QUESTIONS

"What happens to Scout in To Kill a Mockingbird*?"*

"What do the other characters in Julius Caesar *think about Caesar?"*

"How does Hester Prynne in The Scarlet Letter *remind me of my sister?"*

---

2. COLLECT EVIDENCE

Once you know what question you want to answer, it's time to scour the book for things that will help you answer the question. Don't worry if you don't know what you want to say yet—right now you're just collecting ideas and material and letting it all percolate. Keep track of passages, symbols, images, or scenes that deal with your topic. Eventually, you'll start making connections between these examples, and your thesis will emerge.

Here's a brief summary of the various parts that compose each and every work of literature. These are the elements that you will analyze in your essay and that you will offer as evidence to support your arguments. For more on the parts of literary works, see the Glossary of Literary Terms at the end of this section.

ELEMENTS OF STORY These are the *whats* of the work—what happens, where it happens, and to whom it happens.

- **Plot:** All the events and actions of the work.
- **Character:** The people who act and are acted on in a literary work. The main character of a work is known as the *protagonist*.
- **Conflict:** The central tension in the work. In most cases, the protagonist wants something, while opposing forces (antagonists) hinder the protagonist's progress.
- **Setting:** When and where the work takes place. Elements of setting include location, time period, time of day, weather, social atmosphere, and economic conditions.
- **Narrator:** The person telling the story. The narrator may straightforwardly report what happens, convey the subjective opinions and perceptions of one or more characters, or provide commentary and opinion in his or her own voice.
- **Themes:** The main idea or message of the work—usually an abstract idea about people, society, or life in general. A work may have many themes, which may be in tension with one another.

ELEMENTS OF STYLE These are the *hows*—how the characters speak, how the story is constructed, and how language is used throughout the work.

- **Structure and organization:** How the parts of the work are assembled. Some novels are narrated in a linear, chronological fashion, while others skip around in time. Some plays follow a traditional three- or five-act structure, while others are a series of loosely connected scenes. Some authors deliberately leave gaps in their work, leaving readers to puzzle out the missing information. A work's structure and organization can tell you a lot about the kind of message it wants to convey.
- **Point of view:** The perspective from which a story is told. In *first-person point of view*, the narrator involves himself or herself in the story. ("I went to the store"; "We watched in horror as the bird slammed into the window.") A first-person narrator is usually the protagonist of the work, but not always. In *third-person point of view*, the narrator does not participate

in the story. A third-person narrator may closely follow a specific character, recounting that individual character's thoughts or experiences, or it may be what we call an *omniscient* narrator. Omniscient narrators see and know all: they can witness any event in any time or place and are privy to the inner thoughts and feelings of all characters. Remember that the narrator and the author are not the same thing!

- **Diction:** Word choice. Whether a character uses dry, clinical language or flowery prose with lots of exclamation points can tell you a lot about his or her attitude and personality.
- **Syntax:** Word order and sentence construction. Syntax is a crucial part of establishing an author's narrative voice. Ernest Hemingway, for example, is known for writing in very short, straightforward sentences, while James Joyce characteristically wrote in long, extremely complicated lines.
- **Tone:** The mood or feeling of the text. Diction and syntax often contribute to the tone of a work. A novel written in short, clipped sentences that use small, simple words might feel brusque, cold, or matter-of-fact.
- **Imagery:** Language that appeals to the senses, representing things that can be seen, smelled, heard, tasted, or touched.
- **Figurative language:** Language that is not meant to be interpreted literally. The most common types of figurative language are *metaphors* and *similes*, which compare two unlike things in order to suggest a similarity between them—for example, "All the world's a stage," or "The moon is like a ball of green cheese." (Metaphors say one thing *is* another thing; similes claim that one thing is *like* another thing.)

---

3. Construct a Thesis

When you've examined all the evidence you've collected and know how you want to answer the question, it's time to write your thesis statement. A *thesis* is a claim about a work of literature that needs to be supported by evidence and arguments. The thesis statement is the heart of the literary essay, and the bulk of your paper will be spent trying to prove this claim. A good thesis will be:

- **Arguable.** "*The Great Gatsby* describes New York society in the 1920s" isn't a thesis—it's a fact.

- **Provable through textual evidence.** "*Hamlet* is a confusing but ultimately very well-written play" is a weak thesis because it offers the writer's personal opinion about the book. Yes, it's arguable, but it's not a claim that can be proved or supported with examples taken from the play itself.
- **Surprising.** "Both George and Lenny change a great deal in *Of Mice and Men*" is a weak thesis because it's obvious. A really strong thesis will argue for a reading of the text that is not immediately apparent.
- **Specific.** "Dr. Frankenstein's monster tells us a lot about the human condition" is *almost* a really great thesis statement, but it's still too vague. What does the writer mean by "a lot"? *How* does the monster tell us so much about the human condition?

Good Thesis Statements

Question: In *Romeo and Juliet*, which is more powerful in shaping the lovers' story: fate or foolishness?

Thesis: "Though Shakespeare defines Romeo and Juliet as 'star-crossed lovers,' and images of stars and planets appear throughout the play, a closer examination of that celestial imagery reveals that the stars are merely witnesses to the characters' foolish activities and not the causes themselves."

Question: How does the bell jar function as a symbol in Sylvia Plath's *The Bell Jar*?

Thesis: "A bell jar is a bell-shaped glass that has three basic uses: to hold a specimen for observation, to contain gases, and to maintain a vacuum. The bell jar appears in each of these capacities in *The Bell Jar*, Plath's semi-autobiographical novel, and each appearance marks a different stage in Esther's mental breakdown."

Question: Would Piggy in *The Lord of the Flies* make a good island leader if he were given the chance?

Thesis: "Though the intelligent, rational, and innovative Piggy has the mental characteristics of a good leader, he ultimately lacks the social skills necessary to be an effective one. Golding emphasizes this point by giving Piggy a foil in the charismatic Jack, whose magnetic personality allows him to capture and wield power effectively, if not always wisely."

4. Develop and Organize Arguments

The reasons and examples that support your thesis will form the middle paragraphs of your essay. Since you can't really write your thesis statement until you know how you'll structure your argument, you'll probably end up working on steps 3 and 4 at the same time. There's no single method of argumentation that will work in every context. One essay prompt might ask you to compare and contrast two characters, while another asks you to trace an image through a given work of literature. These questions require different kinds of answers and therefore different kinds of arguments. Below, we'll discuss three common kinds of essay prompts and some strategies for constructing a solid, well-argued case.

Types of Literary Essays

- **Compare and contrast**

  Compare and contrast the characters of Huck and Jim in The Adventures of Huckleberry Finn.

  Chances are you've written this kind of essay before. In an academic literary context, you'll organize your arguments the same way you would in any other class. You can either go *subject by subject* or *point by point*. In the former, you'll discuss one character first and then the second. In the latter, you'll choose several traits (attitude toward life, social status, images and metaphors associated with the character) and devote a paragraph to each. You may want to use a mix of these two approaches—for example, you may want to spend a paragraph apiece broadly sketching Huck's and Jim's personalities before transitioning to a paragraph or two describing a few key points of comparison. This can be a highly effective strategy if you want to make a counterintuitive argument—that, despite seeming to be totally different, the two characters or objects being compared are actually similar in a very important way (or vice versa). Remember that your essay should reveal something fresh or unexpected about the text, so think beyond the obvious parallels and differences.

- **Trace**

  Choose an image—for example, birds, knives, or eyes—and trace that image throughout Macbeth.

  Sounds pretty easy, right? All you need to do is read the play, underline every appearance of a knife in *Macbeth* and then list them in your essay in the order they appear, right? Well, not exactly. Your teacher doesn't want a simple catalog of examples. He or she wants to see you make *connections* between those examples—that's the difference between summarizing and analyzing. In the *Macbeth* example, think about the different contexts in which knives appear in the play and to what effect. In *Macbeth*, there are real knives and imagined knives; knives that kill and knives that simply threaten. Categorize and classify your examples to give them some order. Finally, always keep the overall effect in mind. After you choose and analyze your examples, you should come to some greater understanding about the work, as well as the role of your chosen image, symbol, or phrase in developing the major themes and stylistic strategies of that work.

- **Debate**

  Is the society depicted in 1984 *good for its citizens?*

  In this kind of essay, you're being asked to debate a moral, ethical, or aesthetic issue regarding the work. You might be asked to judge a character or group of characters *(Is Caesar responsible for his own demise?*) or the work itself (*Is* Jane Eyre *a feminist novel*?). For this kind of essay, there are two important points to keep in mind. First, don't simply base your arguments on your personal feelings and reactions. Every literary essay expects you to read and analyze the work, so search for evidence in the text. What do characters in *1984* have to say about the government of Oceania? What images does Orwell use that might give you a hint about his attitude toward the government? As in any debate, you also need to make sure that you define all the necessary terms before you begin to argue your case. What does it mean to be a "good" society? What makes a novel "feminist"? You should define your terms right up front, in the first paragraph after your introduction.

Second, remember that strong literary essays make contrary and surprising arguments. Try to think outside the box. In the *1984* example above, it seems like the obvious answer would be no, the totalitarian society depicted in Orwell's novel is *not* good for its citizens. But can you think of any arguments for the opposite side? Even if your final assertion is that the novel depicts a cruel, repressive, and therefore harmful society, acknowledging and responding to the counterargument will strengthen your overall case.

---

5. Write the Introduction

Your introduction sets up the entire essay. It's where you present your topic and articulate the particular issues and questions you'll be addressing. It's also where you, as the writer, introduce yourself to your readers. A persuasive literary essay immediately establishes its writer as a knowledgeable, authoritative figure.

An introduction can vary in length depending on the overall length of the essay, but in a traditional five-paragraph essay it should be no longer than one paragraph. However long it is, your introduction needs to:

- **Provide any necessary context.** Your introduction should situate the reader and let him or her know what to expect. What book are you discussing? Which characters? What topic will you be addressing?
- **Answer the "So what?" question.** Why is this topic important, and why is your particular position on the topic noteworthy? Ideally, your introduction should pique the reader's interest by suggesting how your argument is surprising or otherwise counterintuitive. Literary essays make unexpected connections and reveal less-than-obvious truths.
- **Present your thesis.** This usually happens at or very near the end of your introduction.
- **Indicate the shape of the essay to come.** Your reader should finish reading your introduction with a good sense of the scope of your essay as well as the path you'll take toward proving your thesis. You don't need to spell out every step, but you do need to suggest the organizational pattern you'll be using.

Your introduction should not:

- **Be vague.** Beware of the two killer words in literary analysis: *interesting* and *important*. Of course, the work, question, or example is interesting and important—that's why you're writing about it!
- **Open with any grandiose assertions.** Many student readers think that beginning their essays with a flamboyant statement, such as "Since the dawn of time, writers have been fascinated by the topic of free will," makes them sound important and commanding. In fact, it sounds pretty amateurish.
- **Wildly praise the work.** Another typical mistake student writers make is extolling the work or author. Your teacher doesn't need to be told that "Shakespeare is perhaps the greatest writer in the English language." You can mention a work's reputation in passing—by referring to *The Adventures of Huckleberry Finn* as "Mark Twain's enduring classic," for example—but don't make a point of bringing it up unless that reputation is key to your argument.
- **Go off-topic.** Keep your introduction streamlined and to the point. Don't feel the need to throw in all kinds of bells and whistles in order to impress your reader—just get to the point as quickly as you can, without skimping on any of the required steps.

---

6. Write the Body Paragraphs

Once you've written your introduction, you'll take the arguments you developed in step 4 and turn them into your body paragraphs. The organization of this middle section of your essay will largely be determined by the argumentative strategy you use, but no matter how you arrange your thoughts, your body paragraphs need to do the following:

- **Begin with a strong topic sentence.** Topic sentences are like signs on a highway: they tell the readers where they are and where they're going. A good topic sentence not only alerts readers to what issue will be discussed in the following paragraphs but also gives them a sense of what argument will be made *about* that issue. "Rumor and gossip play an important role in *The Crucible*" isn't a strong topic sentence because it doesn't tell us very much. "The community's constant gossiping creates an environment that allows false accusations to flourish" is a much stronger topic sentence—

it not only tells us what the paragraph will discuss (gossip) but how the paragraph will discuss the topic (by showing how gossip creates a set of conditions that leads to the play's climactic action).

- **Fully and completely develop a single thought.** Don't skip around in your paragraph or try to stuff in too much material. Body paragraphs are like bricks: each individual one needs to be strong and sturdy or the entire structure will collapse. Make sure you have really proven your point before moving on to the next one.
- **Use transitions effectively.** Good literary essay writers know that each paragraph must be clearly and strongly linked to the material around it. Think of each paragraph as a response to the one that precedes it. Use transition words and phrases such as *however*, *similarly*, *on the contrary*, *therefore*, and *furthermore* to indicate what kind of response you're making.

---

7. Write the Conclusion

Just as you used the introduction to ground your readers in the topic before providing your thesis, you'll use the conclusion to quickly summarize the specifics learned thus far and then hint at the broader implications of your topic. A good conclusion will:

- **Do more than simply restate the thesis.** If your thesis argued that *The Catcher in the Rye* can be read as a Christian allegory, don't simply end your essay by saying, "And that is why *The Catcher in the Rye* can be read as a Christian allegory." If you've constructed your arguments well, this kind of statement will just be redundant.
- **Synthesize the arguments rather than summarizing them.** Similarly, don't repeat the details of your body paragraphs in your conclusion. The readers have already read your essay, and chances are it's not so long that they've forgotten all your points by now.
- **Revisit the "So what?" question.** In your introduction, you made a case for why your topic and position are important. You should close your essay with the same sort of gesture. What do your readers know now that they didn't know before? How will that knowledge help them better appreciate or understand the work overall?

- **Move from the specific to the general.** Your essay has most likely treated a very specific element of the work—a single character, a small set of images, or a particular passage. In your conclusion, try to show how this narrow discussion has wider implications for the work overall. If your essay on *To Kill a Mockingbird* focused on the character of Boo Radley, for example, you might want to include a bit in the conclusion about how he fits into the novel's larger message about childhood, innocence, or family life.
- **Stay relevant.** Your conclusion should suggest new directions of thought, but it shouldn't be treated as an opportunity to pad your essay with all the extra, interesting ideas you came up with during your brainstorming sessions but couldn't fit into the essay proper. Don't attempt to stuff in unrelated queries or too many abstract thoughts.
- **Avoid making overblown closing statements.** A conclusion should open up your highly specific, focused discussion, but it should do so without drawing a sweeping lesson about life or human nature. Making such observations may be part of the point of reading, but it's almost always a mistake in essays, where these observations tend to sound overly dramatic or simply silly.

A+ Essay Checklist

Congratulations! If you've followed all the steps we've outlined, you should have a solid literary essay to show for all your efforts. What if you've got your sights set on an A+? To write the kind of superlative essay that will be rewarded with a perfect grade, keep the following rubric in mind. These are the qualities that teachers expect to see in a truly A+ essay. How does yours stack up?

- ✓ Demonstrates a thorough understanding of the book
- ✓ Presents an original, compelling argument
- ✓ Thoughtfully analyzes the text's formal elements
- ✓ Uses appropriate and insightful examples
- ✓ Structures ideas in a logical and progressive order
- ✓ Demonstrates a mastery of sentence construction, transitions, grammar, spelling, and word choice

Suggested Essay Topics

1. *How does Tyler support Tara in becoming independent of their family?*

2. *Why is learning about bipolar disorder a pivotal moment for Tara?*

3. *Why does Tara's father encourage her to pursue music and drama?*

4. *When Tara receives the Gates Cambridge Scholarship, why does she hide the fact that she was homeschooled?*

5. *How does travel impact Tara's view of the world and of herself?*

Glossary of Literary Terms

ANTAGONIST
: The entity that acts to frustrate the goals of the *protagonist*. The antagonist is usually another *character* but may also be a nonhuman force.

ANTIHERO / ANTIHEROINE
: A *protagonist* who is not admirable or who challenges notions of what should be considered admirable.

CHARACTER
: A person, animal, or any other thing with a personality that appears in a *narrative*.

CLIMAX
: The moment of greatest intensity in a text or the major turning point in the *plot*.

CONFLICT
: The central struggle that moves the *plot* forward. The conflict can be the *protagonist*'s struggle against fate, nature, society, or another person.

FIRST-PERSON POINT OF VIEW
: A literary style in which the *narrator* tells the story from his or her own *point of view* and refers to himself or herself as "I." The narrator may be an active participant in the story or just an observer.

HERO / HEROINE
: The principal *character* in a literary work or *narrative*.

IMAGERY
: Language that brings to mind sense-impressions, representing things that can be seen, smelled, heard, tasted, or touched.

MOTIF
: A recurring idea, structure, contrast, or device that develops or informs the major *themes* of a work of literature.

NARRATIVE
: A story.

NARRATOR

The person (sometimes a *character*) who tells a story; the *voice* assumed by the writer. The narrator and the author of the work of literature are not the same thing.

PLOT

The arrangement of the events in a story, including the sequence in which they are told, the relative emphasis they are given, and the causal connections between events.

POINT OF VIEW

The *perspective* that a *narrative* takes toward the events it describes.

PROTAGONIST

The main *character* around whom the story revolves.

SETTING

The location of a *narrative* in time and space. Setting creates mood or atmosphere.

SUBPLOT

A secondary *plot* that is of less importance to the overall story but that may serve as a point of contrast or comparison to the main plot.

SYMBOL

An object, *character*, figure, or color that is used to represent an abstract idea or concept.

SYNTAX

The way the words in a piece of writing are put together to form lines, phrases, or clauses; the basic structure of a piece of writing.

THEME

A fundamental and universal idea explored in a literary work.

TONE

The author's attitude toward the subject or *characters* of a story or poem or toward the reader.

VOICE

An author's individual way of using language to reflect his or her own personality and attitudes. An author communicates voice through *tone*, *diction*, and *syntax*.

A Note on Plagiarism

Plagiarism—presenting someone else's work as your own—rears its ugly head in many forms. Many students know that copying text without citing it is unacceptable. But some don't realize that even if you're not quoting directly, but instead are paraphrasing or summarizing, it is plagiarism unless you cite the source.

Here are the most common forms of plagiarism:

- Using an author's phrases, sentences, or paragraphs without citing the source
- Paraphrasing an author's ideas without citing the source
- Passing off another student's work as your own

How do you steer clear of plagiarism? You should always acknowledge all words and ideas that aren't your own by using quotation marks around verbatim text or citations like footnotes and endnotes to note another writer's ideas. For more information on how to give credit when credit is due, ask your teacher for guidance or visit www.sparknotes.com.

Review & Resources

Quiz

1. What is the name of the mountain nearest to the Westover family home?

    A. Doe Ridge
    B. Stallion Pass
    C. Princess Peak
    D. Buck's Peak

2. In what state do Tara's grandparents live over the winter months?

    A. Florida
    B. Arizona
    C. California
    D. Georgia

3. Which of the following is *not* the name of one of Tara's siblings?

    A. Luke
    B. Richard
    C. Tony
    D. Amy

4. What is the first musical production in which Tara has a leading role?

    A. *Annie*
    B. *West Side Story*
    C. *Jesus Christ Superstar*
    D. *Newsies*

5. How does the congregation react the first time Tara sings a solo in church?

   A. They are embarrassed because her singing is so bad
   B. They are embarrassed because she innocently sings a song with suggestive lyrics
   C. They admire the beauty of her voice
   D. They think her singing is beautiful, but discourage her from performing in the future

6. How does Shawn's head injury impact his behavior?

   A. He continues to be violent and unpredictable
   B. He becomes much calmer and gentler
   C. He is no longer able to concentrate on schoolwork, which frustrates him
   D. He becomes less interested in women and dating

7. What subject does Tara struggle with the most when preparing for her ACT exam?

   A. French
   B. Spanish
   C. Grammar
   D. Trigonometry

8. What type of accident leads to Tara taking Shawn to the hospital?

   A. A motorcycle accident
   B. Severe burns
   C. A fall from construction equipment
   D. A fall from a horse

9. What term does Tara reveal she has never heard after she starts her college education?

   A. Marijuana
   B. Hispanic
   C. Holocaust
   D. Intercourse

10. What information helps Tara to strongly improve her grades during her first year?

    A. Learning that she is expected to read the textbook
    B. Learning that she should review materials before the exam
    C. Learning that lectures and tutorials cover different materials
    D. Learning that she should take notes during lectures

11. What requirement makes Tara worry about maintaining her scholarship while she's pursuing her bachelor's degree?

    A. She has to demonstrate moral purity
    B. She has to be a faithful member of the church congregation
    C. She has to win a spot on a varsity sports team
    D. She has to maintain a high grade-point average

12. Why does the bishop first call Tara for a meeting?

    A. He hears that she is not interested in marriage
    B. He hears that she is very academically gifted
    C. He sees bruises on her arms and thinks that she might be a victim of abuse
    D. He hears that she has been questioning church doctrine

13. How much money does Tara receive in her first grant?

    A. $1,400
    B. $4,000
    C. $14,000
    D. $40,000

14. What is the name of the woman Shawn marries?

    A. Emily
    B. Sadie
    C. Erin
    D. Audrey

15. What major does Tara initially intend to pursue in college?

    A. Music
    B. Philosophy
    C. Chemistry
    D. Sociology

16. Why does the Westover family business in herbs and salves become very successful?

    A. After helping heal her husband's burns, Faye gets a reputation as a great healer
    B. A local preacher tells the congregation the products are blessed
    C. Tara's academic reputation drives people to her family's business
    D. Richard uses his background in chemistry to develop very effective products

17. What European city does Tara travel to with her Cambridge classmates over spring break?

    A. Paris
    B. Rome
    C. Barcelona
    D. Amsterdam

18. In what city is Tara living when her parents make their final visit to her, and she refuses her father's blessing?

    A. Boston
    B. Cambridge
    C. Salt Lake City
    D. San Francisco

19. Which is true of Tara's experience working on her PhD?

   A. She falls far behind on her work, and it seems like she might not be able to complete it
   B. No matter what, she is always very motivated and on top of her workload
   C. She struggles to complete it because she is interested mostly in teaching, not research
   D. She outperforms her classmates but is always insecure about the quality of her own work

20. What significant milestone coincides with Tara submitting her PhD?

   A. Getting engaged to Drew
   B. Her twenty-seventh birthday
   C. The birth of Tyler's daughter
   D. Her parents' fiftieth wedding anniversary

21. Whose funeral brings Tara back to Buck's Peak at the end of the memoir?

   A. Her mother
   B. Her father
   C. Her grandmother
   D. Shawn

22. Including herself, how many of Tara's siblings complete PhDs?

   A. Two
   B. Three
   C. Four
   D. Five

23. Where does Tara live after completing her PhD?

   A. England
   B. Boston
   C. Rome
   D. Utah

24. What is the only condition under which Tara's mother will meet with her?

    A. With the consent of Tara's father
    B. After Tara has gotten married
    C. After Tara has started to attend church services again
    D. In secrecy, far away from Idaho

25. What does Tara credit as the thing that ultimately helped her become strong enough to break free of her family?

    A. A new religious belief that is more liberal and accepting
    B. Love and support from Drew
    C. The financial support she received during her college years
    D. Her education, and the way it opened her mind and challenged her beliefs

Answer Key

1.D, 2.B, 3.D, 4.A, 5.C, 6.A, 7.D, 8.A, 9.C, 10.A, 11.D, 12.A, 13.B, 14.A, 15.A, 16.A, 17.B, 18.A, 19.A, 20.B, 21.C, 22.B, 23.A, 24.A, 25.D

Suggestions for Further Reading

Bushman, Richard. *Mormonism: A Very Short Introduction.* Oxford, UK: Oxford University Press, 2008.

Evans, G. R. *The University of Cambridge: A New History.* Cambridge: I. B. Tauris, 2009.

Hollbrook, Kate, and Matthew Bowman, eds. *Women and Mormonism: Historical and Contemporary Perspectives*. Salt Lake City: University of Utah Press, 2016.

Karr, Mary. *The Art of Memoir.* New York: Harper Perennial, 2016.

Maran, Meredith, ed. *Why We Write about Ourselves: Twenty Memoirists on Why They Expose Themselves and Others in the Name of Literature*. New York: Plume, 2016.

Vance, J. D. *Hillbilly Elegy.* New York: HarperCollins, 2016.

Walter, Jess. *Ruby Ridge: The Truth and Tragedy of the Randy Weaver Family.* New York: Harper Perennial, 2002.

Notes

Notes

Notes

Notes

Notes

Notes

Notes

Notes

Notes

Notes

Notes

NOTES

Notes